E. E. Hewitt

Dew Drops

Comprising new songs, hymns, etc. for young singers

E. E. Hewitt

Dew Drops

Comprising new songs, hymns, etc. for young singers

ISBN/EAN: 9783744781718

Printed in Europe, USA, Canada, Australia, Japan

Cover: Foto ©Thomas Meinert / pixelio.de

More available books at **www.hansebooks.com**

DEW DROPS:

COMPRISING

NEW SONGS, HYMNS, ETC.

FOR

YOUNG SINGERS,

BY

E. E. HEWITT, JNO. R. SWENEY, and WM. J. KIRKPATRICK.

" My speech shall distil as the dew, as the small rain upon the tender herb, an'
as the showers upon the grass."
" I will be as the dew unto Israel: he shall grow as the lily.". . . .

PHILADELPHIA:
John J. Hood,
1024 Arch Street.

Copyright, 1895, by JOHN J. HOOD.

Price, board covers, 25 cents per copy, mailed: $2.40 per dozen, at store.

S pearly drops adorning
   Fair Hermon's lovely flowers,
Come, Lord, in life's sweet morning,
   Bless thou its rosy hours.

May lesson, song, and story,
   Bright dewdrops from above,
Reflect thy grace and glory,
   And sparkle with thy love.
—E. E. H.

COPYRIGHT NOTICE.

To PRINT, for sale or otherwise, any copyright hymn of this collection, unless written permission shall have been obtained, is an infringement of copyright.

THE PUBLISHER.

DEW DROPS.

Praise Him, Ev'ry Voice.

E. E. HEWITT.
INFANT SCHOOL.
JNO. R. SWENEY.

1. Blossoms of the sunny spring, Praise the Lord, praise the Lord; Summer flow'rs, [your
beauty bring, Praise, oh, praise the Lord. All the golden harvest sheaves, All the
brown and crimson leaves, Precious fruits in autumn stor'd. Praise, oh, praise the Lord.

2. Little snowflakes gently fall, Praise the Lord, praise the Lord, His kind care is
over all, Praise, oh, praise the Lord. Stormy clouds and skies of blue; Spring and
summer, winter too, Join a hymn in full accord, Praise, oh, praise the Lord.

3. Little children of the fold, Praise the Lord, praise the Lord, Singing of his
grace untold, Praise, oh, praise the Lord. All the year his tender love Smiles upon us from above, Let us heed his holy word, Praise, oh, praise the Lord.

CHORUS.

Praise him, ev'ry voice, Ev'ry little heart, rejoice,
Children, sweetly sing Praises to our King.

Copyright, 1892, by Jno. R. Sweney.

In His Temple.

E. E. Hewitt. Wm. J. Kirkpatrick.

1. God is in his holy temple; Praise, oh, praise his name to-day,
And remember that he hears us, When we sing and when we pray.
2. Children sang within the temple, When our Saviour gathered there;
Jesus loved their sweet hosannas, Still may we his blessing share.
3. God is in his holy temple; Let us listen to his word;
Learning more and more of Jesus, Sweetest story ever heard.

CHORUS. *a little faster.*

Praise his name, O sweetly praise him, Gather in his house to-day;

poco ritard.

God is in his holy temple, And he hears us when we pray.

Copyright, 1895, by Wm. J. Kirkpatrick.

ABOUT CHURCH GOING.

Q.—Where did Jesus go when he was twelve years old?
A.—To the church at Jerusalem.
Q.—What did Jesus call it?
A.—My Father's house.
Q.—What did he do there?
A.—He listened to the teaching of the Scriptures, both hearing and asking questions.

Q.—Then must children go to church?
A.—Yes; we must try to do as Jesus did.
Q.—How must we behave there?
A.—We must join in the prayers and hymns, and listen to the preaching.
Q.—How can we learn to understand?
A.—The Bible says, All thy children shall be taught of the Lord.

A Song in the Rain.

E. E. Hewitt. Jno. R. Sweney.

1. Once, when a show'r was ¹falling, There came a sweet refrain; A robin in the ²tree-top, Was singing in the rain. Robins gai-ly ³swinging, ⁴Hark! the glad refrain; Swinging, swinging, Singing in the rain.
2. Teach ⁵me your song, dear robin, The meaning's very plain, To trust our ⁶heav'nly Fath-er, In sunshine, cloud, or rain.
3. When ⁷clouds of trouble gather, Oh, let us not complain; We know that ⁸Jesus loves us, We'll ⁹praise him in the rain.
4. For ⁹God, who makes the weather, Brave hearts, like little ¹¹rob-in, Keep singing in the rain.

Will ¹⁰send blue skies again;

Copyright, 1895, by Jno. R. Sweney.

MOTIONS—Arms raised and brought down with fluttering fingers, rain motion. 2, Point as if to tree at the right. 3, Rocking motion with both arms. 4, Right forefinger uplifted 5, Point to self. 6, Point up. 7, Join finger-tips overhead. 8, Press hands together, looking up 9, Point up. 10, Touch finger tips overhead, separate with waving motion right and left. 11, Point to imagined tree.

ORDER OF EXERCISE NO 1.

Teacher.—Good afternoon, (or morning) dear children.

Children, (rising in unison,) Good afternoon, dear teacher.

In Concert.
Quietly each scholar stands,
With closed eyes, and folded hands.
Every head will humbly bow,
We are seeking Jesus now.
While we speak, he draws so near,
Every loving word he'll hear;
He has taught us what to say;
In his blessed name we pray.

Prayer: Our Father, etc.

Singing, an opening hymn. (See page 5)

Recitation by the School.—1st Sunday in the month, The Creed. 2d Sunday, First four Commandments. 3d Sunday, Finish Commandments. 4th Sunday, Beatitudes.

A Short Prayer, led by the teacher, in simple sentences, repeated by the children.

Offerings

Hymn.—"Before Lesson." Page 30

Teaching.

Birthday Gifts.

Teacher.—The Lord watch between me and thee

Response.—When we are absent one from another.

Sing.

—E. E. Hewitt.

Glory be to Jesus.

E. E. Hewitt.   Chorus by W. J. K.

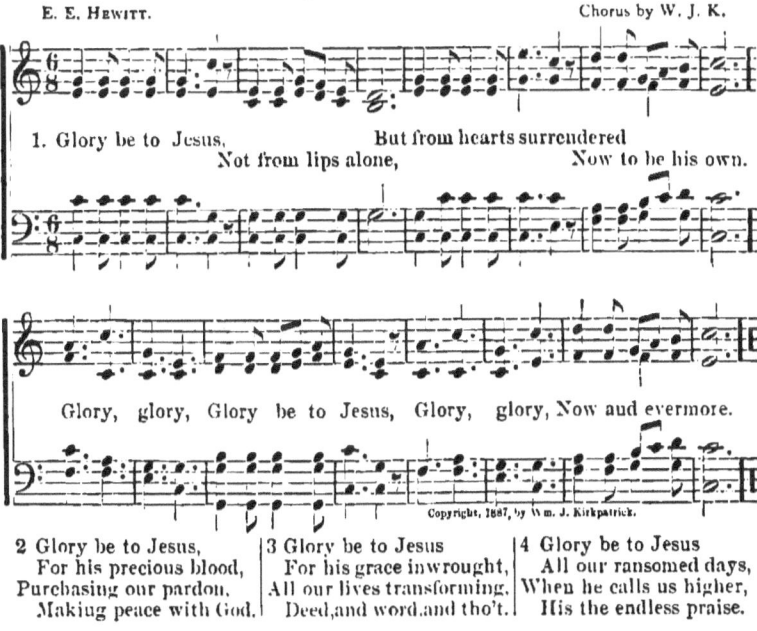

1. Glory be to Jesus, Not from lips alone, But from hearts surrendered Now to be his own.

Glory, glory, Glory be to Jesus, Glory, glory, Now and evermore.

Copyright, 1887, by Wm. J. Kirkpatrick.

2 Glory be to Jesus,
  For his precious blood,
  Purchasing our pardon,
  Making peace with God.

3 Glory be to Jesus
  For his grace inwrought,
  All our lives transforming,
  Deed, and word, and tho't.

4 Glory be to Jesus
  All our ransomed days,
  When he calls us higher,
  His the endless praise.

ORDER OF EXERCISE NO 2.

Teacher.—Good afternoon, dear Children.
Response.
Teacher.—Stand up, and bless the Lord your God.
Response, (with motions.)—Let us lift up our hearts with our hands unto God in the heavens.
Recite, or sing.
  Our Father, on thy throne above,
  All hallowed be thy name of Love;
  Thy kingdom come, thy will be done
  As angels do it, every one.

  Give us our daily bread, this day,
  Forgive our many sins, we pray;
  Help us each other to forgive,
  Lead us, each moment that we live.

  Kept from temptation, evil ways,
  Thine is the kingdom, power and praise;
  Thine is the glory; Lord, again,
  We sing to thee, amen, amen.
Sing.
  Special concert lesson, as Psalm xxiii. Beatitudes, Commandments, Books of the Bible, or other exercise.

Offerings.
Teacher.—What is prayer?
Children.—Prayer is speaking to God, thanking him for his mercies, and asking him for all we need, in the name of the Lord Jesus.
Teacher.—How many of you can think of something for which they want to thank God? (Raise hands.)
Teacher—How many have sickness or trouble in their homes, and would like us to tell "our Father" about it? (Raise hands.)
Children Recite, (with closed eyes, and folded hands,
  God is so good that he will hear
  Whenever children humbly pray;
  He always lends a gracious ear
  To what the youngest child can say.
Short Prayer, by the teacher, repeated in sentences by the school.
Singing.
Lesson.
Closing Exercises.

—F. E. Hewitt.

AN OFFERING EXERCISE.

Teacher.—Remember the words of the Lord Jesus, how he said,

School.—It is more blessed to give than to receive.

Teacher.—Freely ye have received, freely give.

School.—For God loveth a cheerful giver.

Singing; while the offerings are received; see page   Or, the exercise may be varied, by a bright and simple missionary talk by the teacher, or, by a missionary or other appropriate recitation by a scholar.

(The assistants should not count the money during the subsequent exercise, unless they withdraw to another room, as the clink of the coins has a disturbing effect upon the order.

—E. E. Hewitt.

10. All For Jesus.

E. E. Hewitt. Wm. J. Kirkpatrick.

1. Lit-tle hands to work for Je-sus, Lit-tle feet to walk his ways,
2. Lit-tle hands to help each oth-er, Lit-tle lips his grace to tell,
3. Lit-tle eyes to read the sto-ry Of his love in all a-round,
4. Lit-tle lips to speak so gent-ly, Lit-tle knees to bow in prayer,

Lit-tle ears to hear his mes-sage, Lit-tle lips to sing his praise.
Lit-tle songs to raise to heav-en, Lit-tle hearts to love him well.
Lit-tle minds to learn the les-sons In the ho-ly Bi-ble found.
Lit-tle feet to do his er-rands, Lit-tle hearts to trust his care.

CHORUS.

All for Je-sus, all for Je-sus, True and faithful may I be;

All for Je-sus, all for Je-sus, All for him who died for me.

Copyright, 1892, by Wm. J. Kirkpatrick.

First Verse: 1st line, present hands, palms outward; 2d line, step back and forth; 3d line, point to ears; 4th line, to lips. Second Verse: 1st line, all join hands; 2d line, touch lips; 3d line, touch lips, and wave hands upward; 4th line, touch hearts. Third Verse: 1st line, touch eyes; 2d line, wave arms to right and left; 3d line, touch foreheads; 4th line, form book with hands Fourth Verse: 1st line, touch lips; 2d line, knees; 3d line, step; 4th line, touch hearts. Chorus: 1st line, uplift arms, look up; 2d line, point to self; 3d line, same as first; 4th line, point upward; 5, to self,

A Happy Little Home.

E. E. Hewitt. Wm. J. Kirkpatrick.

1. On the bough of the tree, Over there, over there, There's a pretty sight to see, O-ver there, o-ver there. There's a happy lit-tle home, Gently now on tiptoe come, See the happy little home On the bough of the tree.
2. There are two birdies wee, In the nest, in the nest, Mother-bird is coming— see! To her nest, to her nest. Don't disturb her, girls and boys, Do not frighten her with noise, Step off softly, girls and boys, From the old apple-tree.
3. If the wild wind should blow, In the night, in the night; Swing the branches to and fro, In the night, in the night. Who for birdies will take care, 'Neath the green leaves over there, For three birdies who will care, If the wild wind should blow?
4. There's our Father above, Looking down looking down, And his heart is full of love, Looking down, looking down. He will watch o'er you and me, Care for birdies—one, two, three, Let us love him—you and me, Love "our Father" above.

Copyright, 1893, by Wm. J. Kirkpatrick.

First Verse: 1st line, gently rock right arm; 2d and 4th lines, all point in same direction; 5th line, hands together like nest; 6th line, tip-toeing; 7th line, same as 5th; last line, same as first. Second Verse: 1st line, hold up two fingers; 2d line, form nest; 3d line, flight-motion with hands; 4th line, same as 2d; 5th line, hand lifted in warning; 6th line, finger on lip; 7th line, stepping back. Third Verse: 1st line, arms waved overhead; 3d line, decided swinging motion; 6th line, point; 7th line, hold up three fingers. Fourth Verse: 1st and 3d lines, point up; 5th line, point to neighbor, then to self; 6th line, hold up one, two, three fingers; 7th line, hands folded, look up.

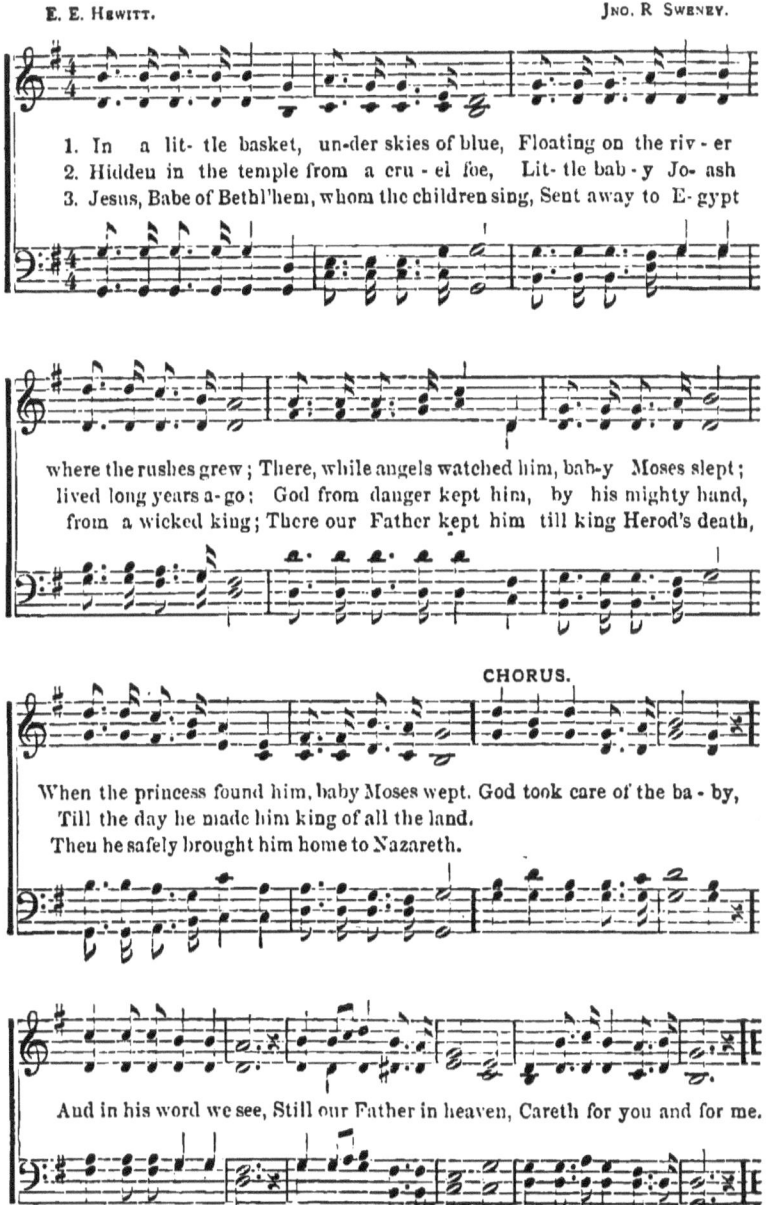

Hosanna We Sing.

G. S. HODGES. Rev. J. B. DYKES.

1. Ho-sanna we sing, like the children dear, In the old-en days when the Lord lived here; He bless'd little children and smil'd on them, While they chanted [his praise in Je-ru-sa-lem. Al-le-lu-ia we sing like the children bright, With their harps of gold, and their raiment white, As they follow their Shepherd with loving eyes Thro' the beautiful valleys of Par-a-dise.

2. Ho-sanna we sing, for he bends his ear, And rejoices the hymns of his own to hear; We know his heart will never wax cold To the lambs that he feeds in his earth-ly fold. Al-le-lu-ia we sing in the church we love; Al-le-lu-ia resounds in the church above; To thy little ones, Lord, may such grace be given, That we lose not our part in the song of heav'n. A-men.

Suffer Them to Come.

J. J. Lowe.

1. I'm but a child, yet Jesus died, From sin to set me free;
2. I must go to him as he said, And he will smile and say:
3. Then I shall know that I am his, And he my Friend and Guide;

"Suf-fer the lit-tle ones," he said, "And let them come to me."
"Come close within my arms, dear child, I'll lead thee all the way."
Though I can lit-tle do for him, I shall be near his side.

CHORUS.

Suffer the children to come unto me, Suffer the children to come unto me;

Suffer them to come, and forbid them not, For of such is the kingdom of heaven.

Copyright, 1895, by Jno. R. Sweney.

THE LORD IS GOOD TO ALL.

THE Lord is good to all, and his tender mercies are over all his works.
While the earth remaineth, seed-time and harvest, and cold and heat, and summer and winter, and day and night shall not cease.
Thou hast made summer and winter.

20. Oh, Come where Love is Bending.

FANNY J. CROSBY.   JNO. R. SWENEY.

1. Oh, come with hearts re-joic-ing, And full of grateful praise, For this re-turning Sab-bath, The best of all our days.
2. Oh, come and learn the Bible, That book whose ev'ry page Is bright with words of comfort, For childhood, youth, and age.
3. Oh, come and learn of Je-sus, Believe and serve him now, Let ev-'ry one be-lieve him, In sweetest rapture bow.
4. Oh, come, and if we ask him He'll take us in his care, And bring us to his king-dom, E-ter-nal life to share.

CHORUS.

Oh, come where love is bend-ing, The chil-dren's song to hear, And Je-sus with his blessing crowns Our Sab-bath home so dear.

Oh, come, yes, come where love is bend-ing, The children's, the chil-dren's song to hear, to hear, And Je-sus, Je-sus . . . Sabbath, Sab-bath

Copyright, 1881, by John J. Hood.

Carry the Light.—CONCLUDED.

CHORUS.

Light! light! beautiful light! Streaming from heaven's fair height; Living for Je-sus, our pre-cious Saviour, Car-ry the beauti-ful light.

Thankful Hearts.

MAY F. WILLIAMS.   JNO. R. SWENEY.

1. Thankful hearts to-day we bring, Dear, loving Saviour; Help us now thy praise to sing, Dear, loving Saviour.
2. In thy tender, watchful care, Dear, loving Saviour; Fold and keep us safely there, Dear, loving Saviour.
3. Nev-er let a naughty word, Dear, loving Saviour; From our youthful lips be heard, Dear, loving Saviour.
4. Train us up to live with thee, Dear, loving Saviour; Where thy glory we shall see, Dear, loving Saviour.

CHORUS.

Keep thy children now, we pray, Ever in the shining way, Lead us gen-tly ev-'ry day, Dear, loving Saviour.

Copyright, 1892, by Jno. R. Sweney.

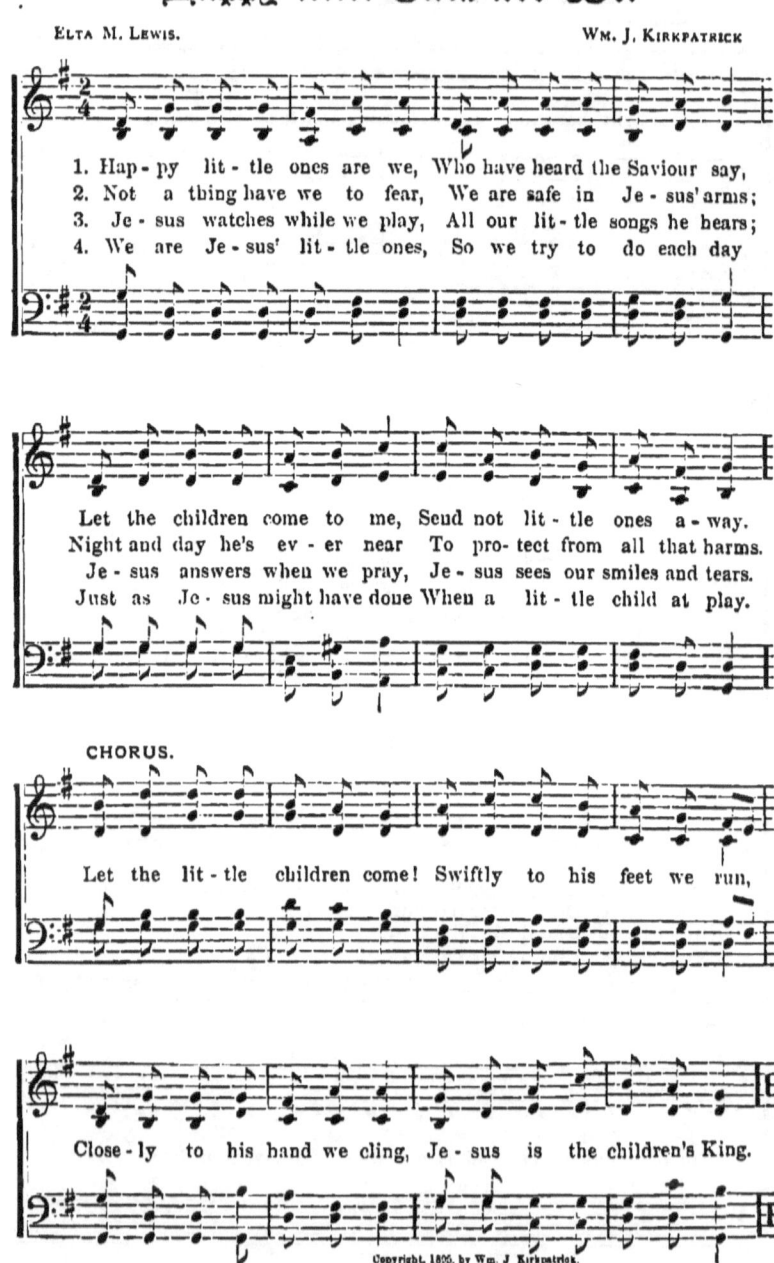

Carrie Ellis Breck.   I. H. Meredith.

1. Je-sus is our blessed King, Un-to whom we glad-ly bring
2. Je-sus is our lov-ing Friend, And his blessing will at-tend
3. Je-sus will our sins for-give, He will teach us how to live,

Cho.—We will love him more and more, Till our earthly days are o'er,

D. C. Chorus.

Hap-py songs we all may sing, Sing with hearts of love.
All who serve him till the end, Serve him ev - er - more.
And a heavenly home will give, Give us by and by.

Till we reach the shin-ing shore, Far be-yond the sky.

Copyright, 1895, by John J. Hood.

JESUS THE ONLY SAVIOUR.

Who is Jesus?
God says: This is my beloved Son in whom I am well pleased.
Why was he named Jesus?
"Thou shalt call his name Jesus: for he shall save his people from their sins." Jesus means, Saviour.
When did he receive this name?
When he was born at Bethlehem, nearly 1900 years ago.
Why did he come into the world?
Christ Jesus came into the world to save sinners.
Was Jesus living before this time?
Yes, in heaven. He was "in the beginning with God."
Is he living now?
Yes, he has gone back to heaven, and says, Behold, I am alive forevermore.
Sing, "The Very same Jesus."
Is Jesus the only Saviour?
"There is none other name under heaven given among men, whereby we must be saved."
Why do we need a Saviour?
Because we are sinners. "All have sinned, and come short of the glory of God."
What does God say of sin?
"The soul that sinneth, it shall die."
What did God do to save us from sin, and its dreadful punishment?
"God so loved the world, that he gave his only begotten Son, that whosoever believeth in him, should not perish, but have everlasting life."
Sing. "For God so Loved the World."
Then "what must I do to be saved?"
"Believe on the Lord Jesus Christ, and thou shalt be saved."
What is meant by believing on Jesus?
It means to give ourselves entirely to him, that he may wash away our sins in his blood, and give us new, loving, and obedient hearts.
Is he able to do this?
"He is able also to save them to the uttermost that come unto God by him."
Is he willing?
He is "not willing that any should perish, but that all should come to repentance."
When should we begin to be sorry for sin, and ask Jesus for salvation?
"Behold, now is the day of salvation."
Will he receive little children who trustfully come to him?
"He took them up in his arms, put his hands upon them, and blessed them."
Sing. "Let them come," page 29.
Will we give ourselves to Jesus to-day? Will we ask him every day to keep us from sin, and make us good and pure? Let us close our eyes, and as many as wish to do so from the heart, say after me these words:

"Just as I am, without one plea,
But that thy blood was shed for me,
And that thou bidst me come to thee,
Dear Lamb of God, I come."

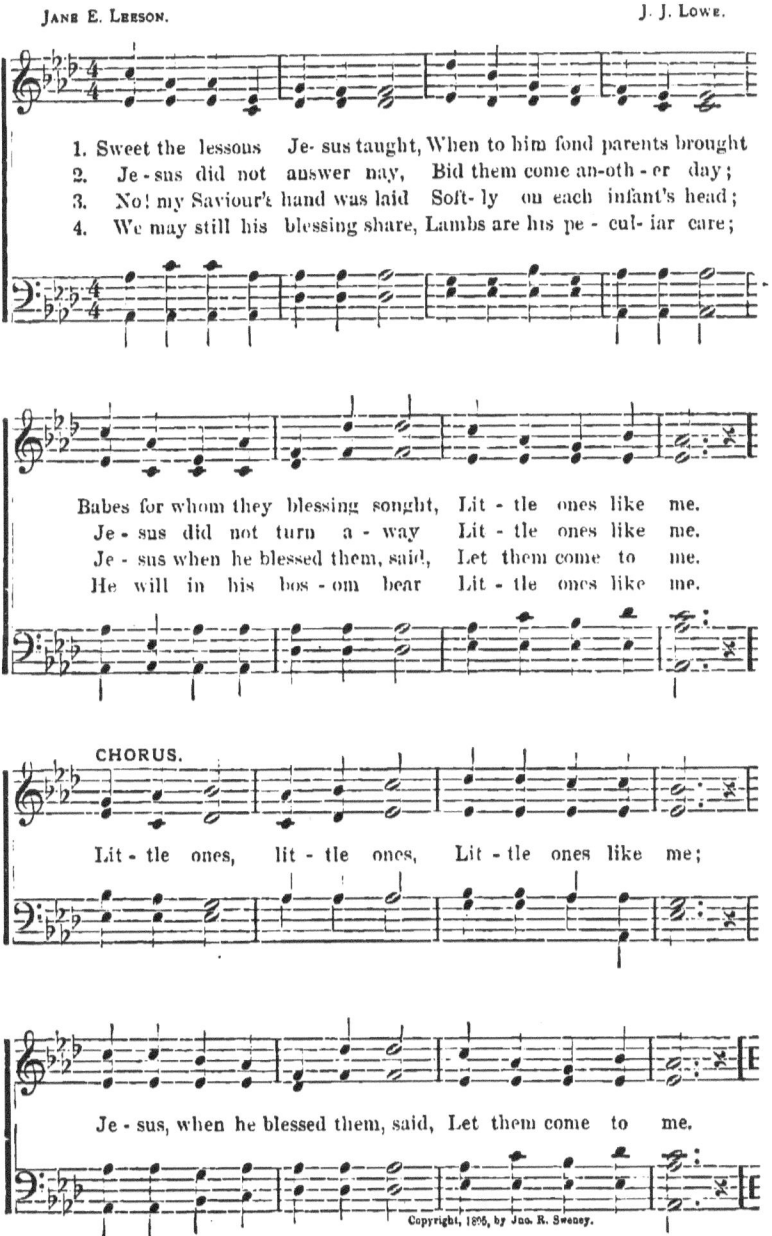

Motion Song Before Lesson.

E. E. HEWITT.   WM. J. KIRKPATRICK.

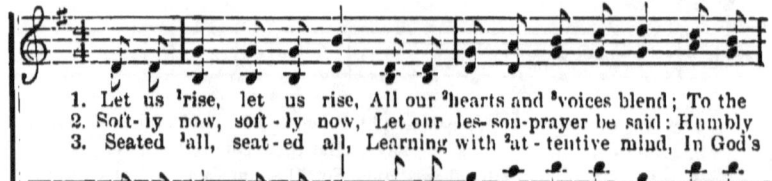

1. Let us ¹rise, let us rise, All our ²hearts and ³voices blend; To the skies, to the skies, May our songs ⁴ascend. Praise to ⁵him who brings us here,
2. Soft-ly now, soft-ly now, Let our les-son-prayer be said: Humbly ¹bow, humbly bow, Ev-'ry lit-tle head. Father, ²bless thy truth, we pray,
3. Seated ¹all, seat-ed all, Learning with ²at-tentive mind, In God's word, in God's word, Blessing we shall find. Move our ³hands and fingers, so!

In our Sabbath home so dear, Hand in ⁶hand, hand in hand, In his house we stand.
Help us live it, day by day; In thy love, in thy love, Teach us from above.
Folded then, ⁴our arms must go, Teacher dear, teacher dear, Ready now to hear.

Copyright, 1893, by Wm. J. Kirkpatrick.

MOTIONS.—First verse, 1, Rise in union. 2, 3, Touch heart, lips. 4, Waft hands higher and higher till fully upraised. 5, Hands pressed together, looking up. 6, Join hands. (Children recite, The title of to-day's lesson is—) Second verse, 1, Bowed heads 2, Clasp hands. (Recite, The Golden Text to-day is—) Third verse, 1, Take seats quietly. 2, Touch foreheads 3, Raise arms, shake hands and fingers. Motion may be varied from time to time. 4, Fold arms. Let the teaching of the lesson follow at once, before the perfect order is at all disturbed.

HEARING AND DOING.

(This little exercise can sometimes be used as a preface to the lesson, instead of the motion hymn, "Before Lesson.")

Signal for rising.

Teacher.—"Come, ye children, hearken unto me: I will teach you the fear of the Lord."

Children.—" Now therefore are we all here present before God."

Teacher.—" Be ye doers of the word, and not hearers only."

Children sing or recite, with motions:

Saviour, draw in mercy near;
Touch our ears that they may hear;
Touch our hearts to love thee still,
And our hands to do thy will.

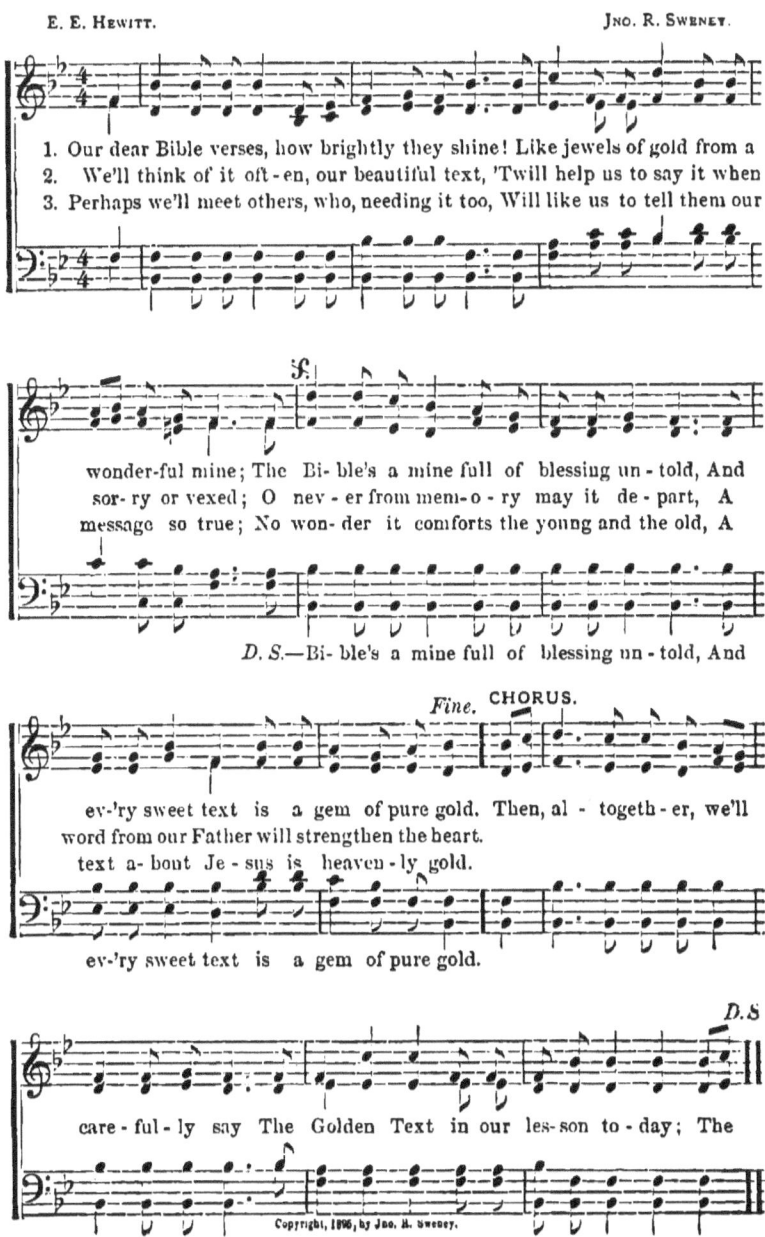

Building on the Rock of Ages.

33

E. E. Hewitt.   Wm. J. Kirkpatrick.

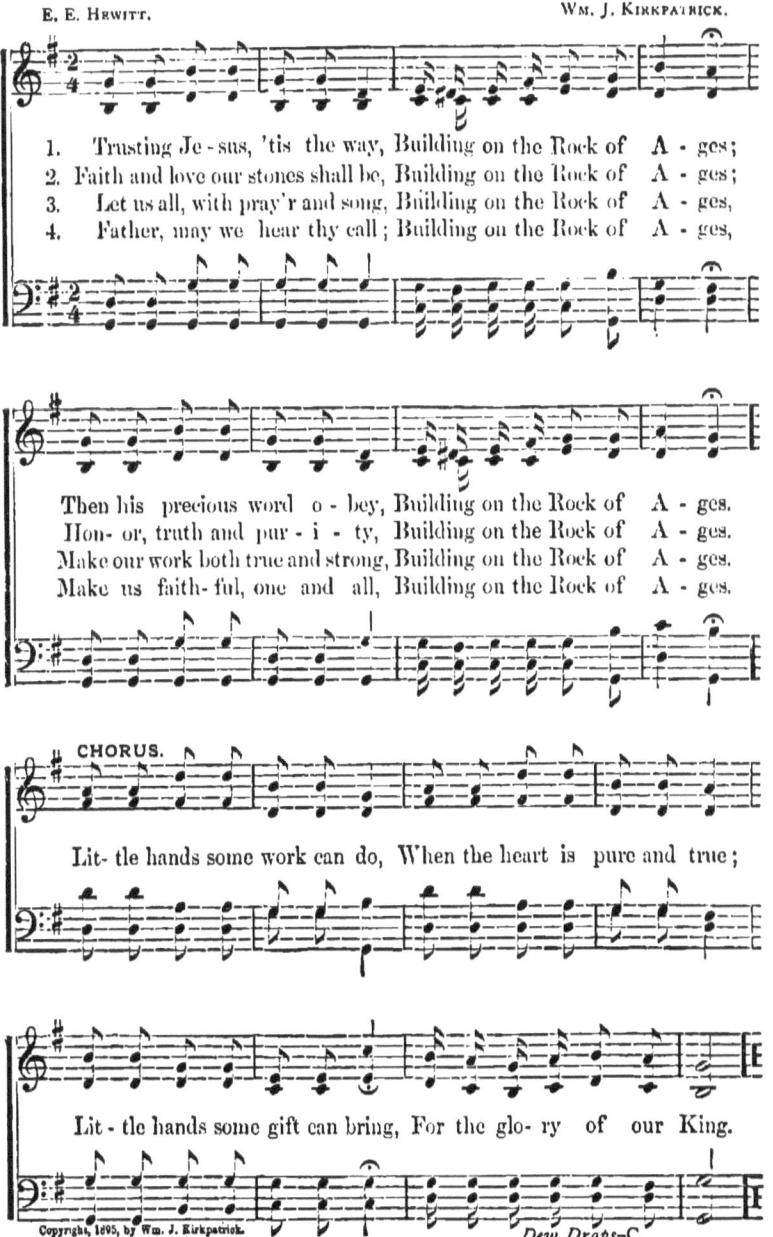

1. Trusting Je-sus, 'tis the way, Building on the Rock of A-ges;
2. Faith and love our stones shall be, Building on the Rock of A-ges;
3. Let us all, with pray'r and song, Building on the Rock of A-ges,
4. Father, may we hear thy call; Building on the Rock of A-ges,

Then his precious word o-bey, Building on the Rock of A-ges.
Hon- or, truth and pur-i-ty, Building on the Rock of A-ges.
Make our work both true and strong, Building on the Rock of A-ges.
Make us faith-ful, one and all, Building on the Rock of A-ges.

CHORUS.

Lit- tle hands some work can do, When the heart is pure and true;

Lit- tle hands some gift can bring, For the glo-ry of our King.

Copyright, 1895, by Wm. J. Kirkpatrick.   *Dew Drops*—C

34. That Sweet Story of Old.

Mrs Jemima Luke.   Arr. by W. J. K.

Slow, with expression.

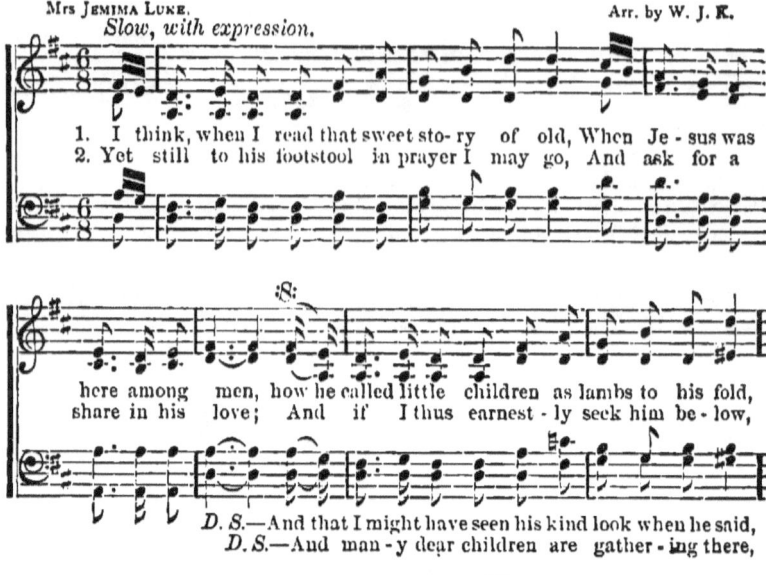

1. I think, when I read that sweet sto-ry of old, When Je-sus was here among men, how he called little children as lambs to his fold, I should like to have been with them then. I wish that his hands had been placed on my head, That his arms had been thrown around me;
2. Yet still to his footstool in prayer I may go, And ask for a share in his love; And if I thus earnest-ly seek him be-low, I shall see him and hear him a-bove. In that beau-ti-ful place he is gone to prepare For all who are washed and forgiven;

D. S.—And that I might have seen his kind look when he said,
D. S.—And man-y dear children are gather-ing there,

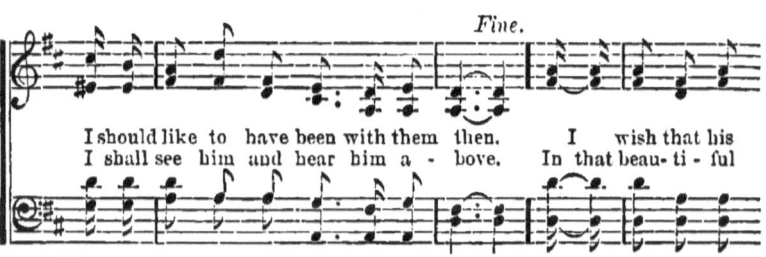

"Let the lit-tle ones come un-to me."
For of such is the kingdom of heaven.

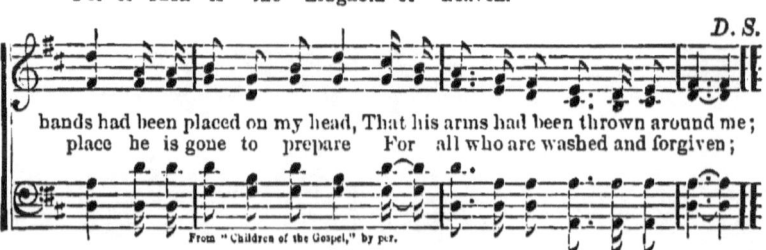

From "Children of the Gospel," by per.

3 But thousands and thousands, who wander and fall,
Never heard of that heavenly home;
I should like to know there is room for them all,
And that Jesus has has bid them to [come.

I long for that blessed and glorious time,
The fairest, and brightest, and best;
When the dear little children of every clime,
Shall come to his arms and be blest.

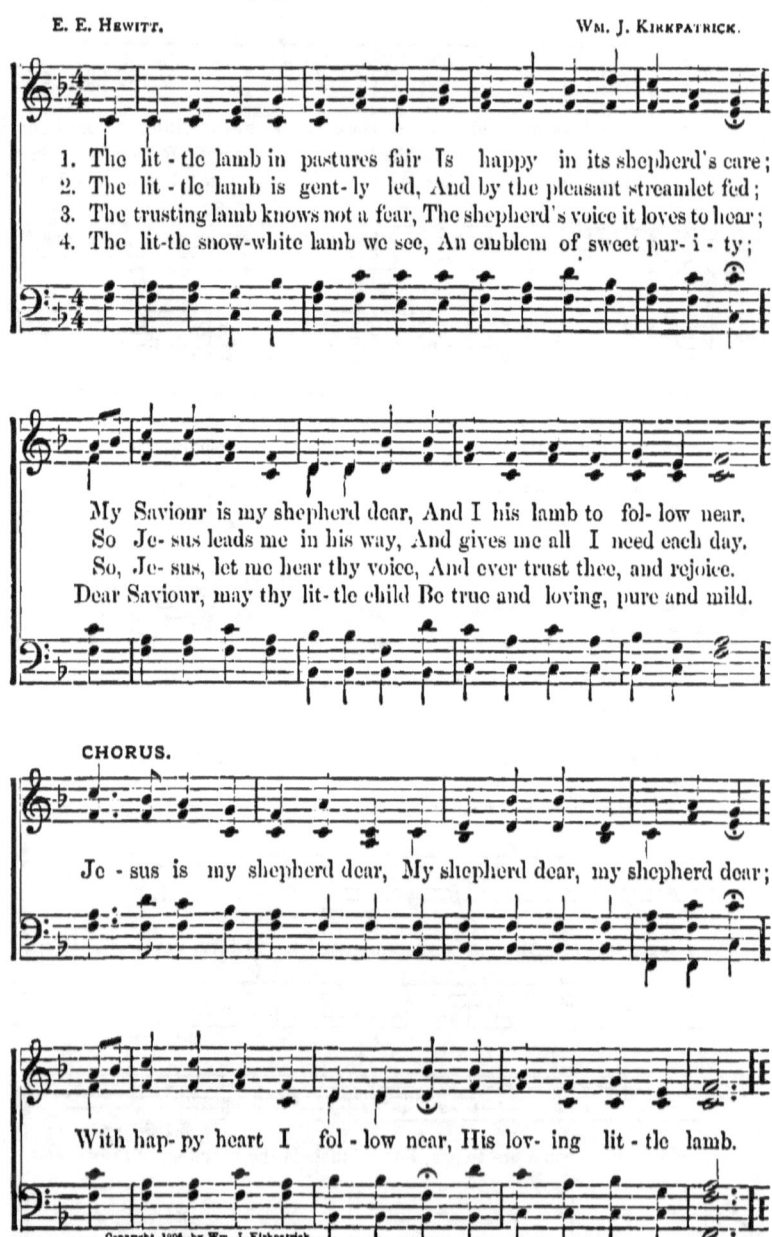

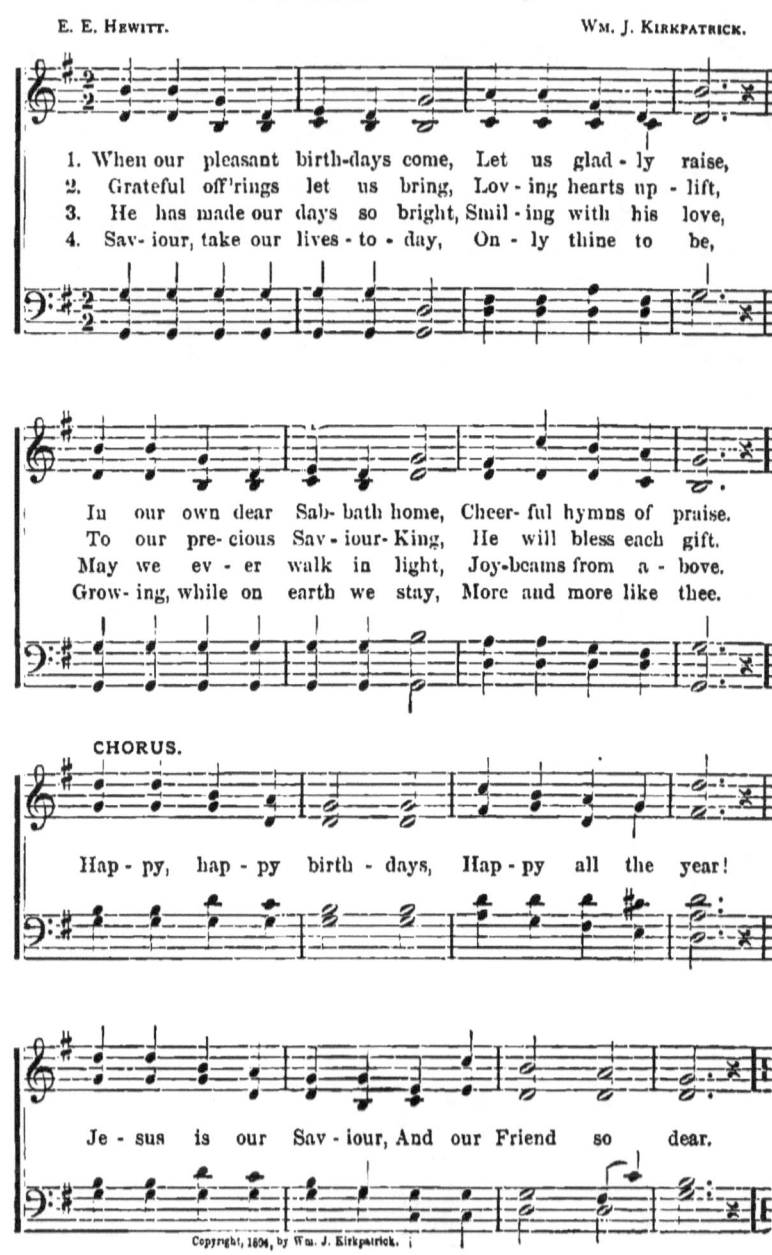

The Birthday Box.

E. E. Hewitt. Wm. J. Kirkpatrick.

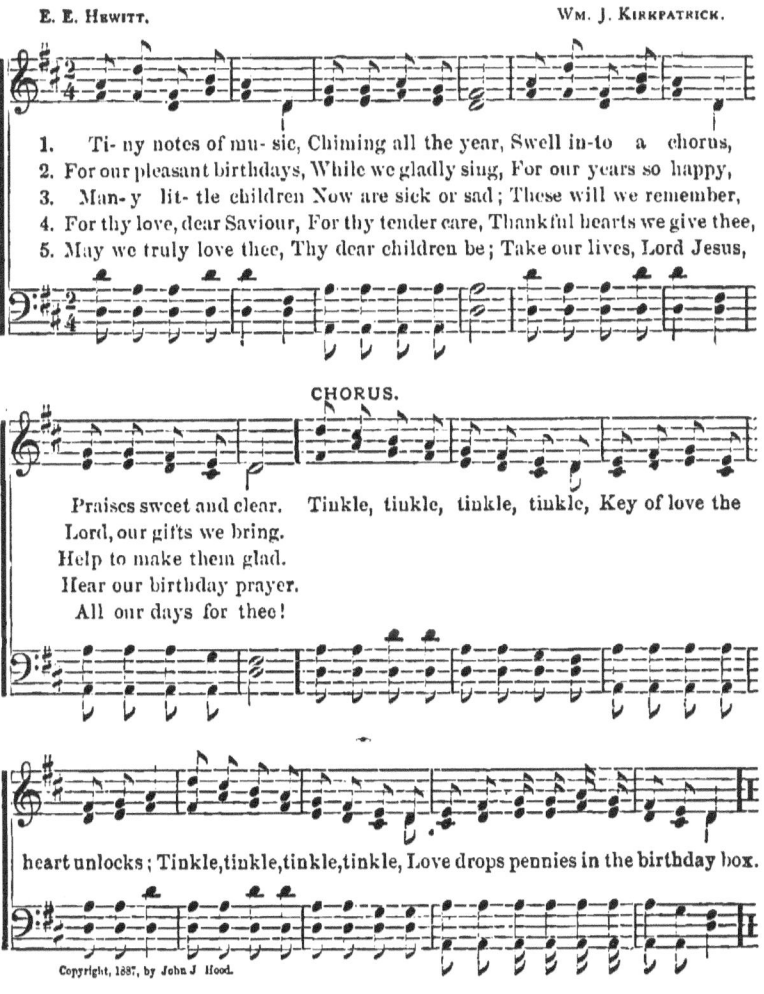

1. Ti- ny notes of mu- sic, Chiming all the year, Swell in-to a chorus,
2. For our pleasant birthdays, While we gladly sing, For our years so happy,
3. Man- y lit- tle children Now are sick or sad; These will we remember,
4. For thy love, dear Saviour, For thy tender care, Thankful hearts we give thee,
5. May we truly love thee, Thy dear children be; Take our lives, Lord Jesus,

Praises sweet and clear.
Lord, our gifts we bring.
Help to make them glad.
Hear our birthday prayer.
All our days for thee!

CHORUS.

Tinkle, tinkle, tinkle, tinkle, Key of love the heart unlocks; Tinkle, tinkle, tinkle, tinkle, Love drops pennies in the birthday box.

Copyright, 1887, by John J. Hood.

BIRTHDAY BOX EXERCISE.

Teacher.—How many children have had birthdays this week?

Children rise and come forward during the singing of a verse or two of a birthday hymn. See pages 40, 41.

Teacher, (as the pennies are dropped, one for each year.) Lucy is five years old, May is eight, Willie is seven. Let us pray. (A few words by the teacher, asking a blessing on the children and their gifts;) or the scholars may rise and recite:

Dear Father, bless our little friends,
 Who bring their birthday gifts to-day;
Watch over them in tender love,
 And guide them in thy holy way.
—E. E. H.

42. Some Little Work for Jesus.

E. E. HEWITT.
JNO. R. SWENEY.

1. Some little work for Jesus The ¹smallest hands can do; Tho' ²shining angels
2. Some little work for Jesus The ¹smallest hands can do; And by ³his grace can
3. Some little work for Jesus The ¹smallest hands can do; O let us seek his

serve him, He needs the children too. He wants their ³hearts to love him, Their
ren - der A ser- vice pure and true. At home, and by the wayside, To
blessing, And ⁶come to him a- new! In these bright days of childhood, Our-

lips to ⁴sing his praise, Their lives to show his glory, In sweet and gentle ways.
⁵scatter flow'rs of love, And help the weary-hearted, To ³trust in God above.
selves to him we give, That we may daily please him, Who died that we might live.

CHORUS.

Some little work for Jesus The ¹smallest hands can do; Some happy work for
Je - sus, Our Friend, so good and true.

MOTIONS.—1, Holding out both hands.
2, Point up.
3, 4, Touch heart, lips.
5, As if scattering flowers.
6, Extending both arms upward.
7, Hands folded on the breast; look up.

Copyright, 1895, by Jno. R. Sweney.

Lessons from the Clock.

E. E. Hewitt. Wm. J. Kirkpatrick.

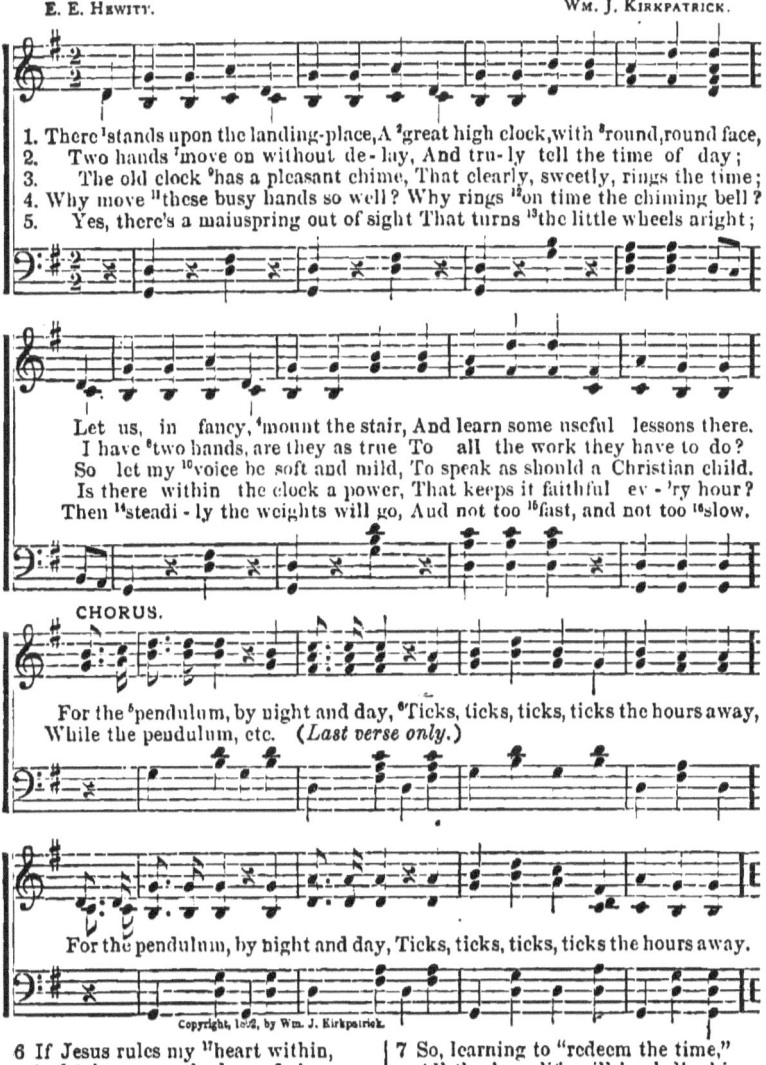

1. There [1]stands upon the landing-place, A [2]great high clock, with [3]round, round face,
2. Two hands [4]move on without de-lay, And tru-ly tell the time of day;
3. The old clock [9]has a pleasant chime, That clearly, sweetly, rings the time;
4. Why move [11]these busy hands so well? Why rings [12]on time the chiming bell?
5. Yes, there's a mainspring out of sight That turns [13]the little wheels aright;

Let us, in fancy, [4]mount the stair, And learn some useful lessons there.
I have [6]two hands, are they as true To all the work they have to do?
So let my [10]voice be soft and mild, To speak as should a Christian child.
Is there within the clock a power, That keeps it faithful ev-'ry hour?
Then [14]steadi-ly the weights will go, And not too [15]fast, and not too [16]slow.

CHORUS.

For the [5]pendulum, by night and day, [6]Ticks, ticks, ticks, ticks the hours away,
While the pendulum, etc. (*Last verse only.*)

For the pendulum, by night and day, Ticks, ticks, ticks, ticks the hours away.

Copyright, 1892, by Wm. J. Kirkpatrick.

6 If Jesus rules my [17]heart within,
And takes away the love of sin;
My [18]hands will work, my [19]feet will move,
My [20]lips will speak, as prompts his love.

7 So, learning to "redeem the time,"
All thro' my life will joy-bells chime,
Oh, [21]happy then the days will be,
That draw me, Saviour, nearer thee.

MOTIONS.—1, Point to supposed landing. 2, Raise right arm, straight and high. 3, Describe circle with hand. 4, Raise right and left feet alternately. 5, Swing right arm across, hanging down 6, Snap thumb and forefinger. 7, Describe circle with two fingers of right hand. 8, Present hands. 9, Bell motion. 10, Touch lips. 11, Circle with two fingers. 12, Bell motion. 13, Turn both hands rapidly, wheel motion. 14, Lower and raise both arms at the side. 15, Right arm moved rapidly up and down. 16, Left arm moved slowly. 17, Touch heart. 18, Present hands. 19, Take step. 20, Touch lips. 21, Clasp hands, look up.

44 Bearing Fruit

"Ye shall know them by their fruits. Do men gather grapes of thorns, or figs of thistles?"
Matthew vii: 16.

F. E. B.   F. E. BELDEN. By per.

1. Little ones may be just like the fruitful trees: Buds are like our tho'ts, which
2. Jesus said, "Ye know them by the fruit they bear;" Words, and looks, and actions
3. Happy are the children who have learned to be Patient, mild and loving,

on-ly Jesus sees, Blossoms are like faces, smiling, clean, and bright;
show just what we are. Bad tho'ts, like the buds of poison fruits and flow'rs,
cheerful, kind, and free; They are trees of promise, bearing fruit of love,

REFRAIN.

Leaves are gentle words, good fruit is do-ing right. Saviour, make us
Yield no pleasant fragrance, cheer no wea-ry hours.
They shall bloom for-ev-er in God's home a-bove.

good and kind like thee, Then each one will be a fruitful tree, Bearing buds and

blossoms, beautiful and sweet, Bearing precious fruit to lay at Jesus' feet.

Copyright, 1892, by F. E. Belden.

To aid in impressing the minds of the children, hold up before them while teaching the second line of the first stanza, a cluster of buds; blossoms, for the third line; leaves and fruit, for the fourth. Unite buds, blossoms, leaves, and fruit while singing last two lines of Refrain. Thistles, nettles, and poisonous plants, flowers, and fruits may be used for last two lines of second stanza.

Hallelujah, Amen.   45

L. H. Edmunds.   Wm. J. Kirkpatrick.

1. Praise ye the Lord, while harps of glory ring, Praise ye the Lord, the
2. Praise ye the Lord, ye mountains and all hills, Wide-rolling sea, and
3. Praise him in darkness, praise him in the light, His is the day, and
4. Praise ye the Lord, who doeth all things well, Sing, children, sing, your

choirs ce- les - tial sing, Praise ye the Lord, from ev - er - lasting, King,
soft-ly-murm'ring rills, Praise him whose love both earth and heaven fills,
his the star - ry night, Praise him for- ev - er, praise him in the height,
glad ho- san- nas swell; Let all who breathe, his great salvation tell,

CHORUS.

Hal - le - lu - jah, a - men. Hal - le - lu - jah, a - men, Hal - le - lu - jah,

a - men, A - men, a - men, Hal - le - lu - jah, a - men.

Copyright, 1895, by Wm. J. Kirkpatrick.

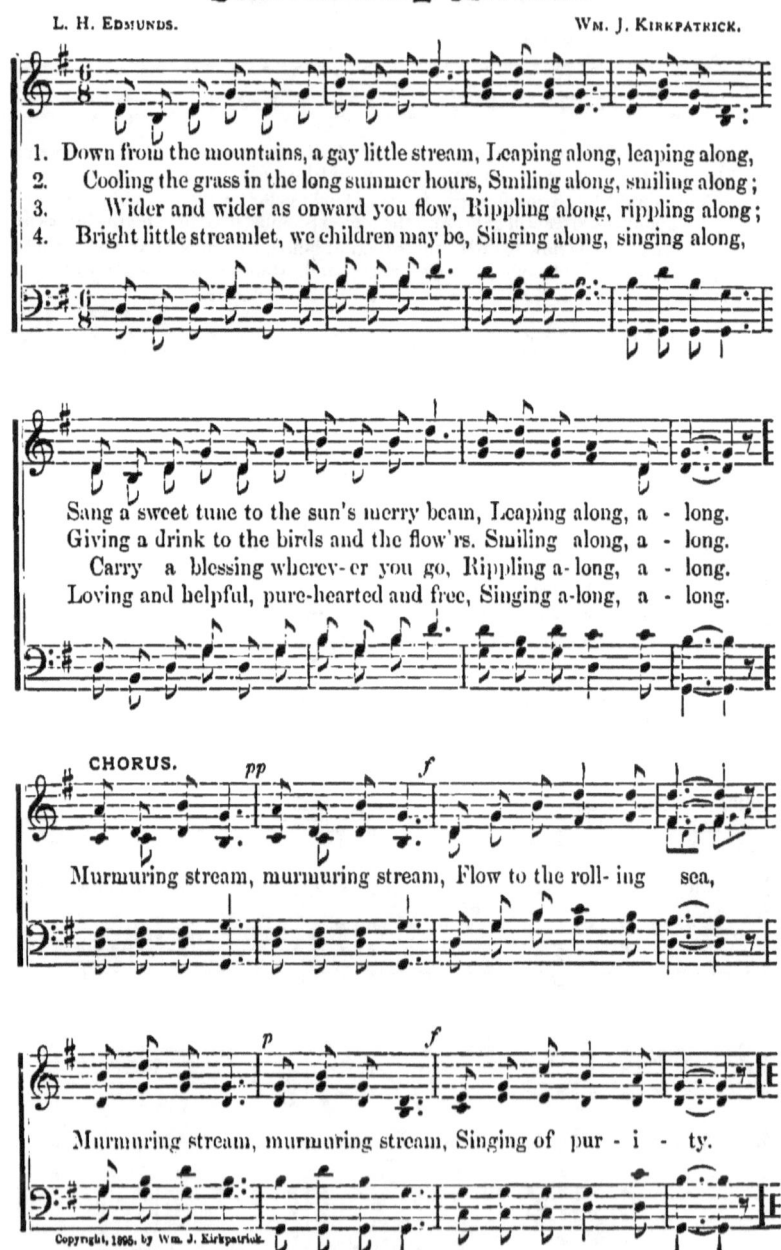

Gentle Shepherd. 51

FANNY J. CROSBY.   JNO. R. SWENEY.

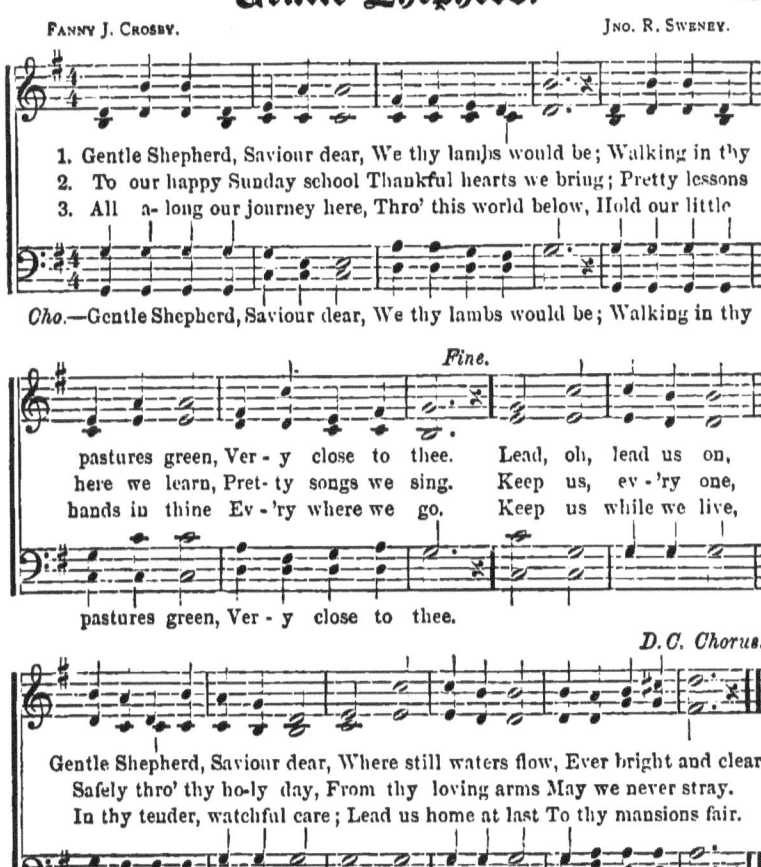

1. Gentle Shepherd, Saviour dear, We thy lambs would be; Walking in thy
2. To our happy Sunday school Thankful hearts we bring; Pretty lessons
3. All a-long our journey here, Thro' this world below, Hold our little

Cho.—Gentle Shepherd, Saviour dear, We thy lambs would be; Walking in thy

pastures green, Ver-y close to thee. Lead, oh, lead us on,
here we learn, Pret-ty songs we sing. Keep us, ev-'ry one,
hands in thine Ev-'ry where we go. Keep us while we live,

pastures green, Ver-y close to thee.

Gentle Shepherd, Saviour dear, Where still waters flow, Ever bright and clear.
Safely thro' thy ho-ly day, From thy loving arms May we never stray.
In thy tender, watchful care; Lead us home at last To thy mansions fair.

Copyright, 1876, by Jno. R. Sweney.

LITTLE FOXES.

Teacher.—Can you say a Bible text about little foxes?
Children—Take us the foxes, the little foxes, that spoil the vines; for our vines have tender grapes.
Teacher.—What is meant by the "little foxes?"
Children.—Wrong ways which we think are only little faults.
T.—What are the tender grapes?
C.—Our young hearts.
T.—What do the little foxes do to the vines?
C.—Spoil the vines.
T.—What do the little faults do?
C.—They injure our souls.
T.—Who can take them away?
C.—The Lord Jesus.
T.—What must we do?
C.—Ask him to save us from all evil.
T.—What else?
C.—We must try, with his help, to overcome our faults.   —E. E. H.

A Bible Exercise. 53

WHAT does the word "Bible" mean?

Bible means "book." The Bible is the Book of books.

Who wrote the Bible?

"Holy men of God."

Who told them what to write?

"They spake as they were moved by the Holy Ghost."

Then how must we receive the Bible?

"Not as the word of men, but as it is in truth, the word of God."

(Singing.) "The Golden Text." p. 31.

How is the Bible divided?

Into the Old and New Testaments; the Old Testament contains 39 books; the New Testament contains 27 books.

Into how many classes are the books of the Old Testament divided?

The books of the Old Testament are divided into five classes; five books of the Law, called Pentateuch; twelve books of history; five books of poetry; five greater books of prophecy; twelve lesser books of prophecy.

Name these books.

The books of the Law are five.
- Genesis,
- Exodus,
- Leviticus,
- Numbers,
- Deuteronomy.

The books of history are twelve.
- Joshua,
- Judges,
- Ruth,
- I Samuel,
- II Samuel,
- I Kings,
- II Kings,
- I Chronicles,
- II Chronicles,
- Ezra,
- Nehemiah,
- Esther.

The books of poetry are five.
- Job,
- Psalms,
- Proverbs,
- Ecclesiastes,
- Song of Solomon.

The greater books of prophecy are five.
- Isaiah,
- Jeremiah,
- Lamentations,
- Ezekiel,
- Daniel.

The lesser books of prophecy are twelve.
- Hosea, Nahum,
- Joel, Habakkuk
- Amos, Zephaniah,
- Obadiah, Haggai,
- Jonah, Zechariah,
- Micah, Malachi.

(Singing.) "Our Bible Story," p. 109.

Into how many classes may the books of the New Testament be divided?

The books of the New Testament may be divided into four classes; four Gospel books, one book of history; twenty-one letters called Epistles, and one book of prophecy.

Name these books.

The four Gospel books are,
- Matthew,
- Mark,
- Luke,
- John.

The book of history is the
- Acts of the Apostles.

The twenty-one Epistles are,
- Romans, Titus,
- I Corinthians, Philemon,
- II Corinthians, Hebrews,
- Galatians, James,
- Ephesians, I Peter,
- Philippians, II Peter,
- Colossians, I John,
- I Thessalonians, II John,
- II Thessalonians, III John,
- I Timothy, Jude.
- II Timothy,

The book of prophecy is,—Revelation.

(Singing.) "Seeking for Me," p. 52.

By what other name is the Bible often called?

The Scriptures; meaning, "writings."

What did Jesus say of the Scriptures?

"Search the Scriptures."

Why?

"They are they which testify of me."

Sing. "More about Jesus," 3rd verse.

How do the Scriptures testify, or speak, of Jesus?

The Old Testament tells us of the Saviour who was to come.

What do the Gospels tell us about Jesus?

The Gospels tell us of his birth, life, and death on the cross for sinners, and of his resurrection and ascension.

What does the book of Acts teach us?

"Acts" teaches us how Jesus carried on his work by his people.

What do the Epistles teach us of Jesus?

They are letters to tell us how to love and serve him.

What does Revelation teach?

It teaches us about the beautiful home in heaven, and the glory of Jesus.

(Singing.) "That Sweet Story," p. 34.

What is the Bible message to children?

Jesus says, Come unto me.

Sing, Come unto Me, the Saviour said.

When must we obey him?

"To-day, if ye will hear his voice, harden not your hearts."

How long will the Bible last?

"The word of our God shall stand forever."

—E. E. H.

A Happy Little Band.

1. See our lit-tle soldier band, Marching on to-day; Keeping time with bus-y feet, And singing all the way. To him who made the world so fair, And taught the birds to sing; We lift again our thankful hearts, And hail the children's [King.
2. Cheer our lit-tle soldier band, Forward still we go; Tho' you think us ver-y small, Our colors we can show. And if you listen, you will hear Our ranks with gladness ring; We love to praise our Saviour's name, And hail the, etc.
3. May our lit-tle soldier band Ev-er faithful be; Keeping close to him who said, O come and learn of me. Then by and by, when angels bright Our welcome song shall sing; We'll clap our hands, and shout aloud, And hail the, etc.

D.C.—We're a happy lit-tle band, Marching on to-day; Looking up with joyful eyes, And singing all the way.

Copyright, 1895, by Jno. R. Sweney.

A HANDFUL OF TEXTS.

One day, when Moses was talking to the people about the words of God's Book, he said, "Bind them for a sign up-on thy hand." God told Moses to say this. Now, how can we bind these words upon our hands? One way, I think, is to let our fingers remind us of some sweet Bible texts. We will learn a text for each finger. The middle finger is the longest you see, so we will "bind" a long text on it. "God so loved the world that he gave his only begotten Son, that whosoever believeth in him should not perish, but have everlasting life."—John iii: 16.

The fourth finger is next. This will help us to remember, "Christ Jesus came into the world to save sinners."1 Tim. i: 15.

Here is a child's text to bind on the forefinger. "Even a child is known by his doings, whether his work be pure, and whether it be right."—Prov. xx: 11.

When men write books, they often leave the children out: but when God made his Book, he did not forget the little ones. Why not? Because he loves them. So here is another child's text, and we will "bind" that on the little finger. "Je-sus called a little child unto him "—Matt. xviii: 2. Do you want to be that little child? You are, because he calls you now. Do you want to answer his call? Here is a little prayer for the thumb, and it will be sweet to use it now—"Lord, help me."

Which is the text for the little finger? the middle finger etc.

—E. E. H.

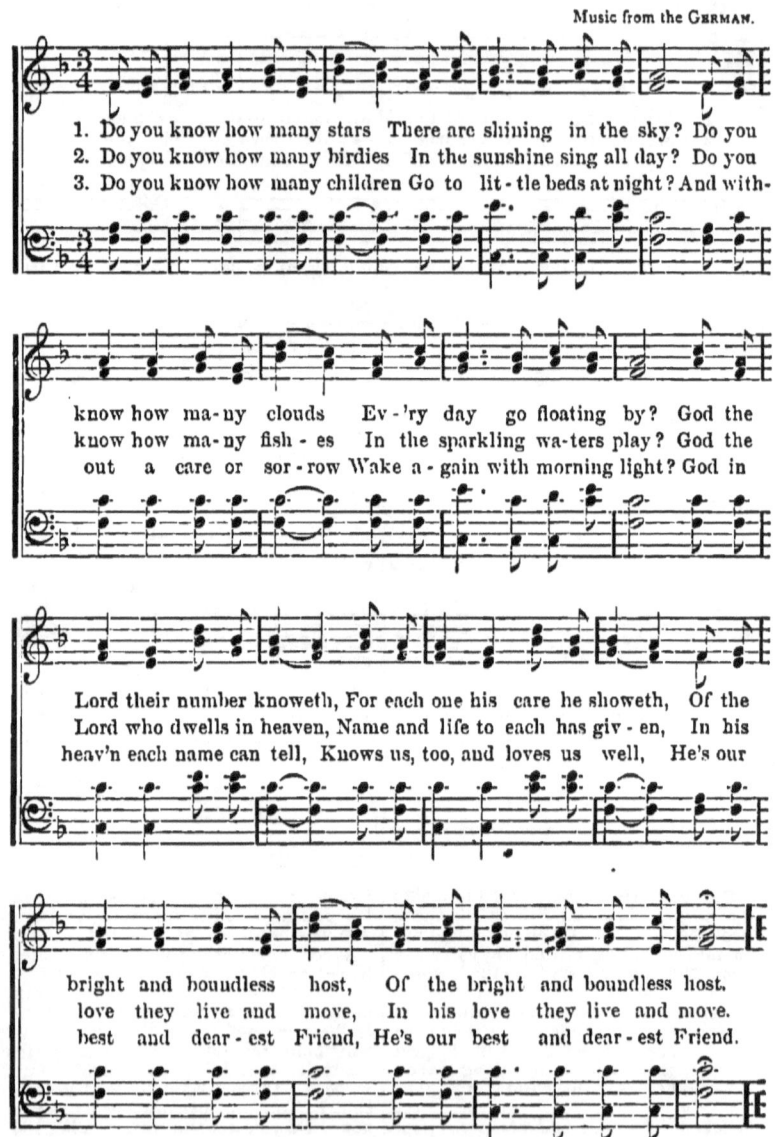

God Knoweth.

Music from the GERMAN.

1. Do you know how many stars There are shining in the sky? Do you know how ma-ny clouds Ev-'ry day go floating by? God the Lord their number knoweth, For each one his care he showeth, Of the bright and boundless host, Of the bright and boundless host.

2. Do you know how many birdies In the sunshine sing all day? Do you know how ma-ny fish-es In the sparkling wa-ters play? God the Lord who dwells in heaven, Name and life to each has giv-en, In his love they live and move, In his love they live and move.

3. Do you know how many children Go to lit-tle beds at night? And with-out a care or sor-row Wake a-gain with morning light? God in heav'n each name can tell, Knows us, too, and loves us well, He's our best and dear-est Friend, He's our best and dear-est Friend.

MOTIONS —VERSE 1. Arms extended above the head; move the fingers to represent the stars. Extend the arms in front and wave the hands, to show clouds. VERSE 2. Extend the arms to the right and left, and move them to imitate the flying of birds. Extend the hands and move from right to left in front to represent fishes. VERSE 3. Bow the head on the hands and shut the eyes, opening them at the words, "Wake again."

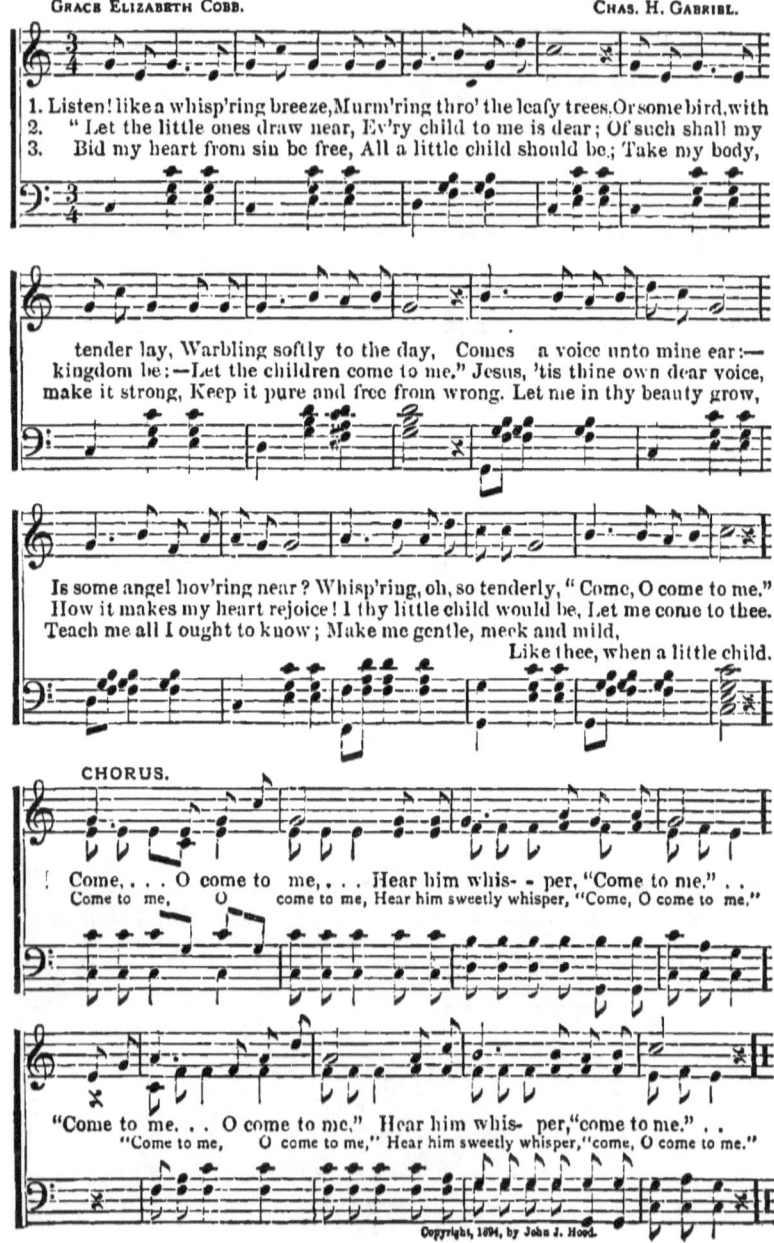

Gentle Jesus.

JNO. R. SWENEY.

1. Gen-tle Je-sus, meek and mild, Look up-on a lit-tle child;
2. Fain I would to thee be brought; Gracious God, for-bid it not;
3. Put thy hands up-on my head, Let me in thine arms be stayed;
4. Fain I would be as thou art; Give me thine o-bedient heart;

Pit-y my sim-plic-i-ty, Suf-fer me to come to thee.
Give me, O my God, a place In the kingdom of thy grace!
Let me lean up-on thy breast, Lull me there, O Lord, to rest.
Thou art pit-i-ful and kind; Let me have thy lov-ing mind.

CHORUS.

Gen-tle Je-sus, meek and mild, Look up-on a lit-tle child.

Copyright, 1895, by Jno. R. Sweney.

THE GOOD SHEPHERD.

Who will be our Shepherd true,
Keeping us life's journey through?
"The Lord is my Shepherd; I shall not want."

2 Who, in pastures green will feed,
And by gentle waters lead?
"He maketh me to lie down in green pastures; he leadeth me beside the still waters."

3 Who will seek the lambs astray,
Bring them to his own right way?
"He restoreth my soul; he leadeth me in the paths of righteousness for his name's sake."

4 Who in loving arms will fold
Little lambs, and kindly hold?
"He shall gather the lambs with his arm, and carry them in his bosom."

5 If in Jesus we rejoice,
Will we know his tender voice?
"The sheep follow him, for they know his voice."

6 Will he call me by my name,—
Jesus, evermore the same?
"He calleth his own sheep by name."

7 What can make his lambs as white
As the snowflakes in his sight?
"The blood of Jesus Christ his Son, cleanseth us from all sin."

8 Will he bear us on his breast,
To the folds forever blest?
"Fear not, little flock; for it is your Father's good pleasure to give you the kingdom." —E. E. H.

66 — Loves You and Me.

WM. T. JONES.   JNO. R. SWENEY.

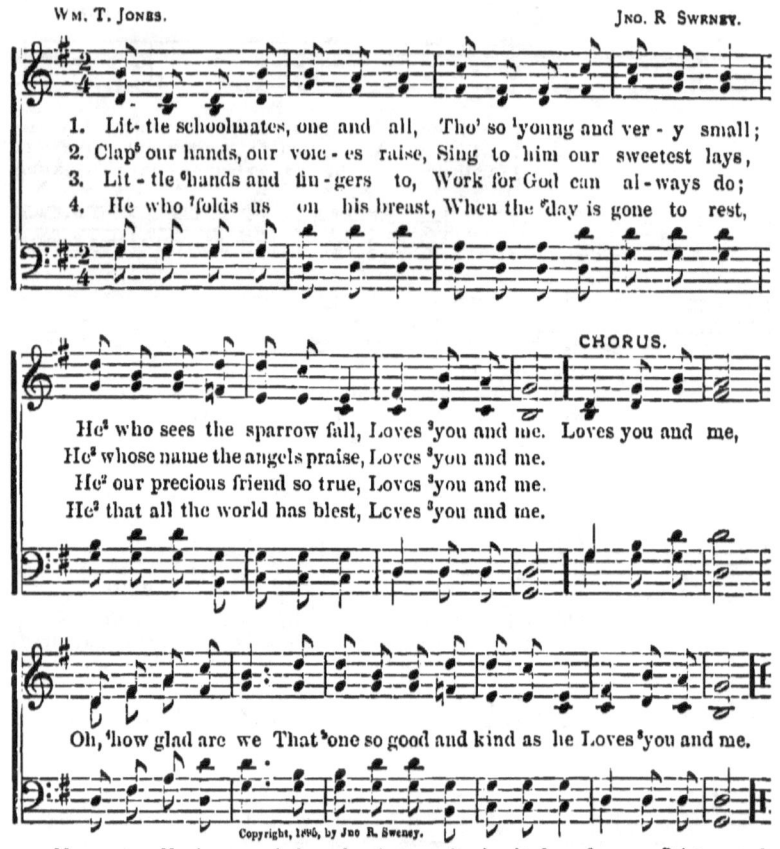

1. Lit- tle schoolmates, one and all, Tho' so ¹young and ver - y small;
2. Clap⁵ our hands, our voic - es raise, Sing to him our sweetest lays,
3. Lit - tle ⁶hands and fin - gers to, Work for God can al - ways do;
4. He who ⁷folds us on his breast, When the ⁸day is gone to rest,

He² who sees the sparrow fall, Loves ³you and me. Loves you and me,
He² whose name the angels praise, Loves ³you and me.
He² our precious friend so true, Loves ³you and me.
He² that all the world has blest, Loves ³you and me.

Oh, ¹how glad are we That ³one so good and kind as he Loves ³you and me.

Copyright, 1886, by Jno R. Sweney.

MOTIONS.—1, Hand outstretched as though measuring height from floor. 2, Point upward. 3, Points to the little one next to her, and then to herself. 4, Hands on the heart. 5, Clap the hands. 6, Both hands outstretched. 7, Hands crossed on breast. 8, Palms of hands together, and head laid on the back of them.

LESSONS FROM THE BIRDS.

LEADER.—Behold the fowls of the air: for they sow not, neither do they reap, nor gather into barns; yet your Heavenly Father feedeth them. Are ye not much better than they?   Matt vi: 26

RESPONSE.—Are not five sparrows sold for two farthings, and not one of them is forgotten before God?

LEADER.—But even the very hairs of your head are all numbered. Fear not therefore: ye are of more value than many sparrows.

RES.—Seek not ye what ye shall eat, or what ye shall drink, neither be ye of doubtful mind.

LEADER.—For all these things do the nations of the world seek after; and your Father knoweth that ye have need of these things.

RES.—But rather seek ye the kingdom of God; and all those things shall be added unto you.

All for Thee. 67

E. E. Hewitt.
Jno. R. Sweney.

1. The little ¹birds are singing for Jesus, The ²flow'rs are blooming for him;
2. The ³sunbeams bright are shining for Jesus, For him the ⁵breezes will blow;
3. Far more than ¹birds, or blossoms, or sunbeams, Can children honor their King;

The golden ³stars, like beautiful angels, Look down thro' shadows dim.
And ⁶rippling streams, in valley and mountain, To happy music flow.
Our ⁷hearts can love our wonderful Saviour, Our lives their service bring.

CHORUS.

Birds and flowers and stars and sunbeams, All, ⁴dear Saviour, all for thee;

And the children's lov-ing prais-es, All, ⁴dear Saviour, all for thee.

Copyright, 1886, by Jno. R. Sweney.

MOTIONS.—1, Flight motion, both hands. 2, Point down. 3, Point up. 4, Both arms raised. 5, Wave arms. 6, Wave motion. 7, Right hand on heart.

JESUS LOVES THE CHILDREN.

QUESTION.—Does Jesus love the children still?
ANSWER.—"Jesus Christ, the same yesterday, to-day, and forever."
QUESTION.—What is his loving word to you to-day?
ANS.—"I love them that love me, and those that seek me early shall find me." *Prov. viii: 17.*
QUESTION.—Has Jesus a place for the children in his heavenly temple?
ANS.—"In heaven their angels do always behold the face of my Father which is in heaven." *Sing "Loves You and Me," p. 66.*

It was Night in the Temple.

E. E. Hewitt.   Jno R Sweney.

1. It was night in the temple, All the lamps burning low, When a voice called to Samuel, In the long, long a-go: 'Twas our Father in Heaven, Spoke in tones soft and clear, And the child heard and answered,
2. In the temple so ho-ly, On the sweet Sabbath day, God, our Father, is speaking, Let us hear and o-bey: For he calls us to Je-sus, To his ways good and true, And to each little ser-vant
3. Yes, our Father is speaking; In the Book of his love There are words full of blessing, That will lead us a-bove: Let us listen so glad-ly To this wonderful Word; Let our actions show plainly

CHORUS.

"Speak, O Lord, for I hear." Speak, dear Father, to me, And thy servant I'll be; Help me do all thy bidding, Make me faithful to thee.
He'll give something to do.
That his children have heard.

Copyright, 1806, by Jno. R. Sweney.

The Child Jesus. 69

(Intended for eight little girls. 1st, in recitation, 2nd, in song, followed by full chorus, 3rd, in recitation, and so on to the close. Recite verses 1, 3, 5, 7, sing 2, 4, 6, 8. No interludes; pianist, after each recitation, strike the pitch of F, and succeeding girl sings: Let the chorus be sung with vigor.)

1ST, RECITATION.

When Jesus was a little child,
In Nazareth of Galilee,
The early lessons of his youth,
Were learned at Mary's knee.

C. H. G. CHAS. H. GABRIEL.

2nd—I love to hear about the Lord, When he was but a little child;
Of how he spent his ear-ly years, So pure and un-de-filed.

CHORUS. *entire school.*

O Je-sus, Saviour of the world, We love to hear and sing of thee;
No oth-er name is dear as thine, Nor ev-er-more shall be.

Copyright, 1891, by John J. Hood.

3 They had no books as we have now,—
No written laws were in the land;
No blessed Bible like our own,
Had he to understand.

4 To do the Father's holy will,
The Saviour left his home above,
And to the earth he brought the light,
Of everlasting love.

5 In Jewish schools the children sat
In little rows upon the ground,
While Rabbis, learned in sacred law,
The scriptures would expound.

6 He came to teach the way of life,—
To spread the knowledge of the truth,
And not to learn the Rabbis' lore,
As Jews required in youth.

7 So thus in wisdom Jesus grew,
In favor both of God and man,
In sweet accordance to the word
Of his eternal plan.

8 The world in superstition lay,
The poor were ev'rywhere denied;
And 'twas that they might have the light,
That Jesus came and died.

Hear the Joyful Carols.

E. E. Hewitt.   Jno R Sweney.

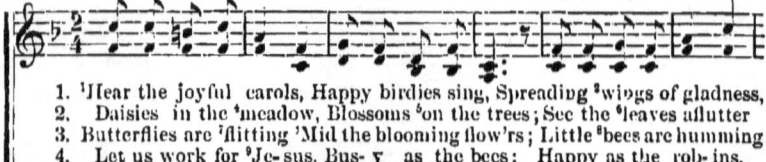

1. Hear the joyful carols, Happy birdies sing, Spreading wings of gladness,
2. Daisies in the meadow, Blossoms on the trees; See the leaves aflutter
3. Butterflies are flitting 'Mid the blooming flow'rs; Little bees are humming
4. Let us work for Jesus, Bus-y as the bees; Happy as the rob-ins,

CHORUS.

In the golden spring. Hark! hark! hark! All the sunny days,
In the gentle breeze.   We will join our
Thro' the pleasant hours.
Sing sweet melodies.

voices To the hymn of praise

MOTIONS.—1, Head bent, and forefinger raised, as in listening. 2, Arms raised, hands rising and falling like wings. 3, Touch lips, and waft hand upward. 4, Point to ground. 5, Raise arm, swing hand from wrist. 6, Raise both arms, shake hands and fingers. 7, Move right hand about, fluttering forefinger. 8, Move left hand about, fluttering forefinger. 9, Point up.

Copyright, 1895, by Jno. R. Sweney.

THE CHILDREN WHO SANG HOSANNA.

QUESTION.—Did Jesus receive the praises of children?
BOYS.—When the chief priests and scribes saw the wonderful things that he did, and the children crying in the temple, and saying, "Hosanna to the Son of David," they were sore displeased, and said unto him, "Hearest thou what they say?"
GIRLS.—And Jesus saith unto them, "Yea, have ye never read, out of the mouths of babes and sucklings, thou hast perfected praise?"
                                                                     Matt xxi: 15, 16

PRAISE THE LORD.

LEADER.—Praise the Lord, O Jerusalem; praise thy God, O Zion.
RESPONSE.—For he hath strengthened the bars of thy gates; he hath blessed thy children within thee.
LEADER.—Praise ye the Lord. Praise ye the Lord from the heavens;
RES.—Praise him in the heights.
LEADER.—Both young men, and maidens,
RES.—Old men, and children. Let them praise the name of the Lord for his name alone is excellent, his glory is above the earth and heaven

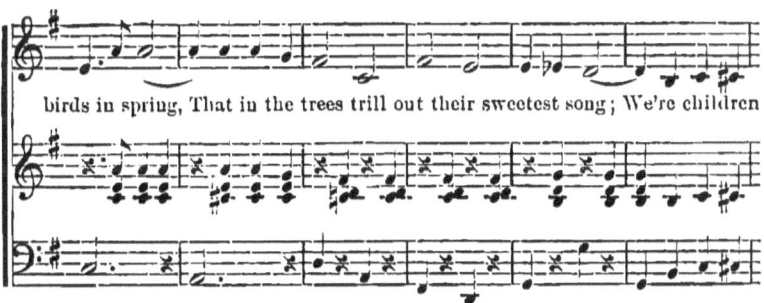

birds in spring, That in the trees trill out their sweetest song; We're children

Repeat chorus, girls singing words, boys whistling melody.

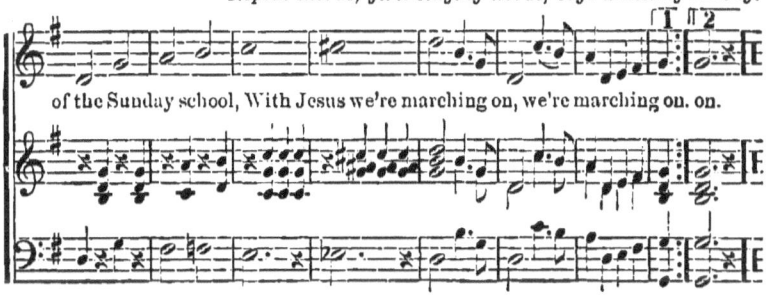

of the Sunday school, With Jesus we're marching on, we're marching on, on.

COMING TO JESUS.

There is a sweet little word of four letters, used many times in the Bible. I will put it on the board. COME. Who is it says, "Come unto me?" Yes, the Lord Jesus. To whom does he say "come?" Everybody? Yes, for there is a text that says, Whosoever will—how many can finish that text for me? Do you think "whosoever" means little children, as well as big people? Yes, of course it does, but to make us even more sure, Jesus kindly said something for the little ones alone. Tell me the children's text. "Suffer the little children to come unto me, and forbid them not, for of such is the kingdom of God." Now, let us sing a verse or two. "In the Days of Old." Page 35

How can we come to Jesus?

We can speak to him from our hearts, saying, "Lord Jesus, I am coming to thee, help me."

Will he hear?

Yes, for he says, him that cometh to me, I will in no wise cast out.

When can we come to Jesus?

Now, for he says, Those that seek me early shall find me. Sing, "Come to Jesus, Just Now."

Here is a picture. (Showing card or drawing.) Yes, a baby just old enough to learn to walk. It does not know how to begin. But mama will stand very near, and say, "come," and hold out her arms, and baby takes one little tottering step, right into mama's arms. So we hear Jesus speaking in his Word. What does he say? "Come unto me." Then, if we are willing, you remember, "whosoever will," we say our little prayer to him from our hearts, and Jesus is so very, very near, this first step takes us into his loving arms.

How many want to take that first step now? Tell Jesus.

Let us bow our heads, and silently whisper to the dear Saviour that we come to him, and ask him to take away our sins, and make us his forever.

Sing, "It Fills my Heart with Joy."

—E. E. H.

78. Stepping in the Light.

L. H. Edmunds.   W. J. Kirkpatrick.

1. Trying to walk in the steps of the Saviour, Trying to follow our
2. Pressing more closely to him who is leading, When we are tempted to
3. Walking in footsteps of gen-tle forbearance, Footsteps of faithfulness,
4. Trying to walk in the steps of the Saviour, Upward, still upward we'll

Saviour and King; Shaping our lives by his blessed ex-am-ple,
turn from the way; Trusting the arm that is strong to defend us,
mer-cy, and love, Looking to him for the grace free-ly promised,
fol-low our Guide, When we shall see him, "the King in his beauty."

CHORUS.

Happy, how happy, the songs that we bring. How beautiful to walk in the
Happy, how happy, our praises each day.
Happy, how happy, our journey above.
Happy, how happy, our place at his side.

steps of the Saviour, Stepping in the light, Stepping in the light; How

beautiful to walk in the steps of the Saviour. Led in paths of light.

Copyright, 1890, by Wm. J. Kirkpatrick.

We Thank Thee.

79

E. E. Hewitt. Jno. R. Sweney.

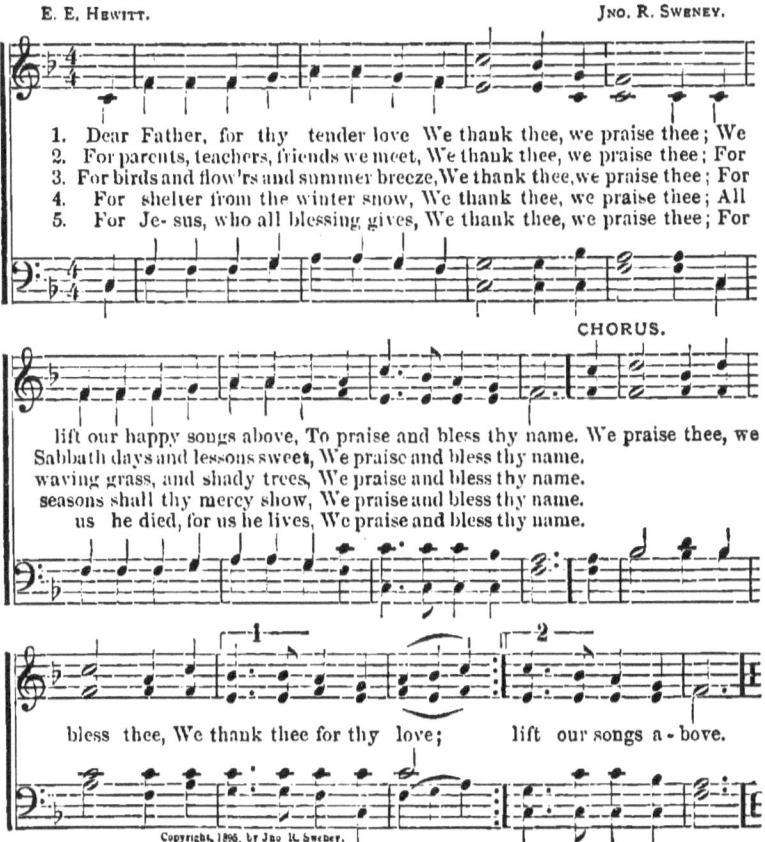

1. Dear Father, for thy tender love We thank thee, we praise thee; We
2. For parents, teachers, friends we meet, We thank thee, we praise thee; For
3. For birds and flow'rs and summer breeze, We thank thee, we praise thee; For
4. For shelter from the winter snow, We thank thee, we praise thee; All
5. For Jesus, who all blessing gives, We thank thee, we praise thee; For

CHORUS.

lift our happy songs above, To praise and bless thy name. We praise thee, we
Sabbath days and lessons sweet, We praise and bless thy name.
waving grass, and shady trees, We praise and bless thy name.
seasons shall thy mercy show, We praise and bless thy name.
us he died, for us he lives, We praise and bless thy name.

bless thee, We thank thee for thy love; lift our songs a-bove.

Copyright, 1896, by Jno R. Sweney.

STEPPING IN THE LIGHT.

What did we talk about last Sunday? About coming to Jesus.

Yes, and I hope many of you did take that "step." But after we step to Jesus, we must step along after him. The baby, you know, (showing picture,) does not stop with that first step,—what must it do? Yes, take another, and another, till it can walk a long way. So we must learn to "walk in the steps of the Saviour." Let us think what that means. How many of you have been to the seashore? Did you not see footprints in the sand? Or, in the winter, you have seen tracks in the fresh snow. You could put your feet in these tracks, and follow after the person who went before you. So the dear Lord Jesus was a child one time, just as old as you are, and he left a child's steps that his children could see and walk in them. He honored his mother, and earthly father—steps of obedience; he was gentle and kind—steps of love; he came to the Temple, and thought of the Heavenly Father—steps of praise.

Remember, dear children, when we do the opposite of these things, when we are unkind, untruthful, irreverent,—we have stepped away from Jesus, we are not walking in his footprints, then. Is it not dreadful to go away from him, into sin and danger?

Let us bow our heads, and ask Jesus to take our hands, and lead us in his own beautiful steps. Then we will sing, "Stepping in the Light." —E. E. H.

Pleasing Jesus.

"For even Christ pleased not himself."

E. E. Hewitt.
Jno. R. Sweney.

1. Let us ask the gracious Sav-iour For a spir-it like his own,
2. "Even Christ," the blessed Mas-ter, Did not seek himself to please,
3. Let us come to him, re-memb'ring That his life our pattern is;
4. Pleasing not ourselves but oth-ers, Pleasing him whose steps we see;

Love in ev-'ry thought and ac-tion, Love in ev-'ry word and tone.
And his love, still watching o'er us, Careth for "the least of these."
So our hearts, to him sur-rendered, Shall be more and more like his.
O what joy to hear him say-ing, Ye have done it un-to me.

CHORUS.

Pleas-ing not ourselves, but Jesus, Let us walk as he shall bid;
Pleasing, pleasing

Pleas-ing not ourselves, but Je-sus, Try to live as Je-sus did.
Pleasing, pleasing

Copyright, 1895, by Jno. R. Sweney.

Missionary Band.

"Go ye therefore, and teach all nations."—Matt. xxviii: 19.

MARY IRENE McLEAN. A. F. MYERS.

Not too fast.

1. We are but a band of children, We are few, and weak, and small,
2. There are man-y lit-tle children, Far a-way a-cross the sea,
3. So we want to send them teachers, Who will teach them how to pray,
4. It was Je-sus died to save them, 'Twas for this to earth he came,

But we want to work for Jesus, And there's work enough for all.
Who have nev-er heard of Je-sus, But to i-dols bend the knee.
To the dear and lov-ing Saviour, Who will wash their sins away.
He will make them pure and hap-py, When they learn to love his name.

CHORUS.

We are a Mission-a-ry Band, Missionary Band, Missionary Band,
We are a Mission-a-ry Band, Do-ing all we can.

5 'Tis the Bible that will lead them,
From the darkness into light,
And we all are glad to help them
Break away from heathen night.

6 Cheerfully we give our pennies,
And we really like the plan,
For we are little missionaries,
Doing all the good we can.

From the "Search Light" by per.

Little Hands can Serve Him.

E. M. Lewis.   Jno. R. Sweney.

1. Lit-tle hands can serve him, Lit-tle feet can go On the Saviour's er-rands, Quickly to and fro.
2. We can car-ry flow-ers To the sick and sad; We can sing of Je-sus, Making oth-ers glad.
3. We can love each oth-er, Quarrels we can shun; We can help an-oth-er, That's the best of fun.
4. We can love the Sav-iour, This is best of all; Let us quickly an-swer, When we hear his call!

CHORUS.
Oh, there's plen-ty to do For you and for me, And so we are hap-py As children can be!

Copyright, 1895, by Jno. R. Sweney.

SENDING THE LIGHT.

Singing. "The Mission Band." Page 82.

(*The questions can be asked by the boys and answered by the girls, or vice versa.*)

Q.—What light can we send to the lands far away, [gospel day? Who know not the joy of the glad
A.—Oh, send the Bible, the book of God's love;
'Twill carry them sunshine from heaven above.
Q.—And what says the Bible, that scatters the night? [great light."
A.—"The people in darkness have seen a
Q.—Who takes them the message that Jesus will save? [brave.
A.—The good missionaries, faithful and
Q.—And who'll give the money, all wrapt up in prayer? [share.
A.—We children are willingly doing our

Q.—And what shall be done with the money we bring [King?
To tell of our Jesus, and honor our
A.—They'll build schools and churches afar o'er the sea, [ren may be,.
And hospitals too, where sick child-
The banner of love on the mountains unfurled, [the world.
They'll take the good tidings all over
Q.—And when we gather, by and by, Who'll meet us there,beyond the sky?
A.—Oh, some from China and Japan, The lands of silk and tea;
And some from coral isles,where grow The palm and bread-fruit tree;
And some from India's crowded plain; Some from Alaska's snow,
But all will sing the same glad song, The same dear Saviour know.

Singing. "Carry the Light." Page 22.

84. The Boys and Girls for Jesus.

E. E. Hewitt.   Jno. R. Sweney.

1. The boys and girls for Jesus, the children's blessed Friend, His love is warm and tender, a love that has no end; And so we gather 'round him, with glad hosannas still, As long ago, the children who sang on Zion's hill.
2. The boys and girls for Jesus, we take him for our Guide, And turn away from evil, the sins for which he died; We take him for our pattern, to serve him all our days, And follow in his footsteps, in wisdom's pleasant ways.
3. The boys and girls for Jesus, the Holy Child was he; His lovely life at Naz'reth, shows us what we should be; Obedient to his parents, to ev'ry duty true, As pure as snowy lilies, as gentle as the dew.

CHORUS.

The boys and girls for Jesus, our happy voices sing, We love him, we trust him, our everlasting King; While over us in triumph the crimson

Copyright, 1895, by Jno. R. Sweney.

The Boys and Girls, etc.—CONCLUDED.

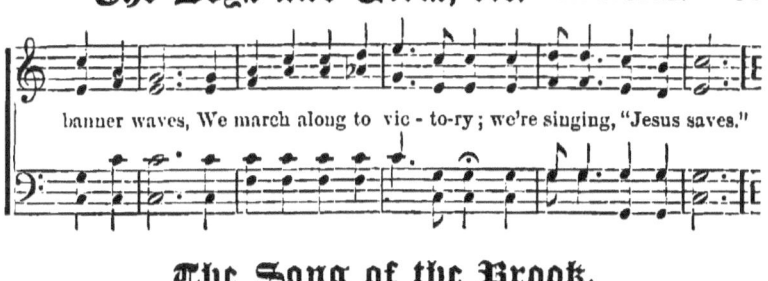

banner waves, We march along to vic-to-ry; we're singing, "Jesus saves."

The Song of the Brook.

MAY S. WILLIAMS. JNO. R. SWENEY.

1. Oh, list to the brook, the bright little brook, That merrily glides along;
2. It sings to the flow'rs, the beautiful flow'rs, It sings to the laughing breeze,
3. The bright little brook is singing for us, And these are the words that fall;

From morn till night, and from night till morn, 'Tis singing its cheerful song.
And wakes the bird in its greenwood home, High up in the waving trees.
Do good, do good wherev-er you can, Do good, and be kind to all.

CHORUS. *f*

Hear it say, as it trips a-way, Down the hill,

pp

murmuring still; I am trying some good to do, Why, why should not you?

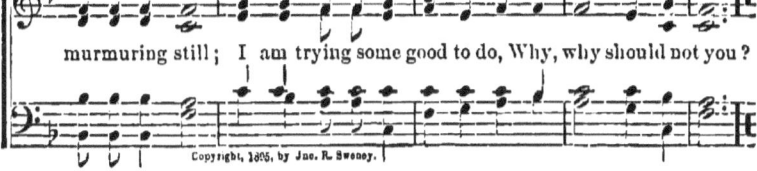

Copyright, 1885, by Jno. R. Sweney.

Sabbath Day.

87

E. E. Hewitt.   Jno. R. Sweney.

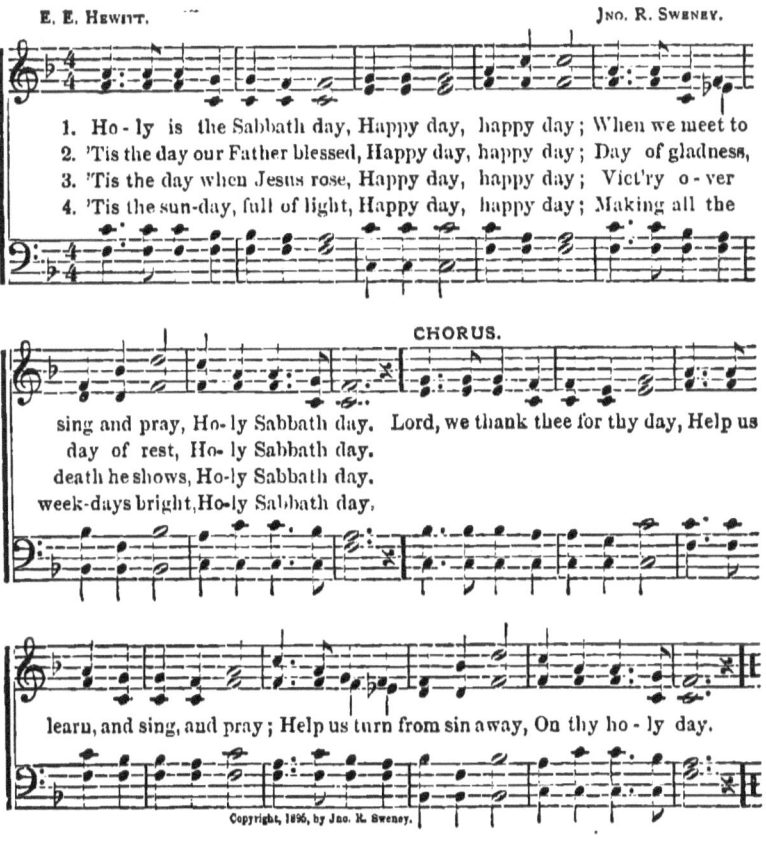

1. Ho-ly is the Sabbath day, Happy day, happy day; When we meet to sing and pray, Ho-ly Sabbath day.
2. 'Tis the day our Father blessed, Happy day, happy day; Day of gladness, day of rest, Ho-ly Sabbath day.
3. 'Tis the day when Jesus rose, Happy day, happy day; Vict'ry o-ver death he shows, Ho-ly Sabbath day.
4. 'Tis the sun-day, full of light, Happy day, happy day; Making all the week-days bright, Ho-ly Sabbath day.

CHORUS.

Lord, we thank thee for thy day, Help us learn, and sing, and pray; Help us turn from sin away, On thy ho-ly day.

Copyright, 1896, by Jno. R. Sweney.

THE SABBATH DAY.

Q.—In all the week, which day's the best?
A.—The day that God our Father blessed, And called the "Sabbath," meaning "rest."
Q.—What does the Fourth Commandment say?
A.—"Remember thou the Sabbath day," God's holy word we must obey.
Q.—Why did our Father give this day?
A.—Because we need it on life's way.
Q.—How did our Saviour, when below, His reverence for the Sabbath show?
A.—He went to church, the Scriptures taught, And deeds of love and mercy [wrought.
Q.—And is it "rest," his word to hear?
A.—Oh, yes; for Jesus then is near, And when we come to be his guest, Our hearts in him can sweetly rest.
Q.—When Jesus rose, and went to heaven, What name was to the Sabbath given?
A.—Disciples met to praise and pray, And called the Sabbath, "the Lord's Day."
Q.—Why keep "the first day of the week?"
A.—Because, when Mary came to seek (On that first morning of the week,) Her Saviour, who for sinners bled, She found him risen from the dead.
Q.—We call the Lord's Day, Sunday, too, And can we find a meaning true?
A.—Like sunbeams, shining clear and bright, [light. The Sundays come with heavenly

—E. E. H.

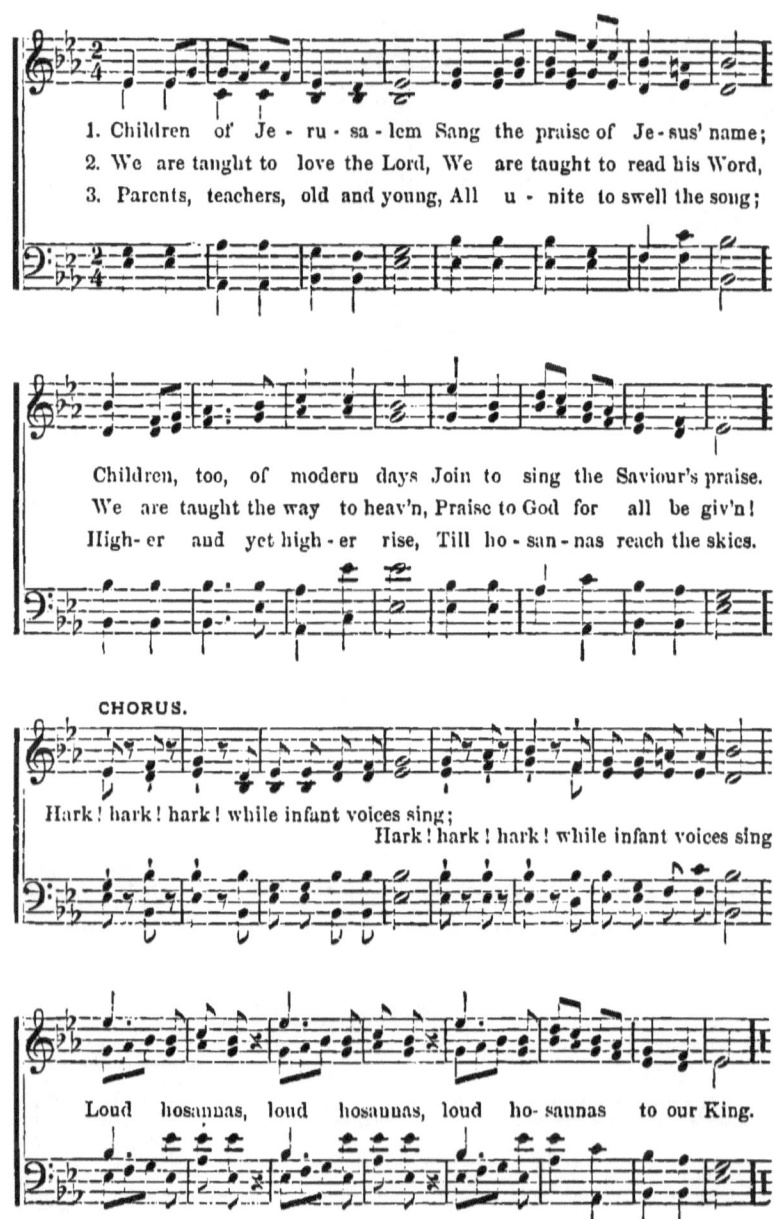

The Children's Prayer.

FANNY J. CROSBY.   JNO. R. SWENEY.

1. Saviour, ¹grant the children's pray'r, Fold and keep us in thy care;
2. May our ⁷feet, from day to day, Swiftly run the narrow way;
3. May ¹²we love and serve thee well, May we live, that we may dwell

Cho.—Saviour, ¹grant the children's pray'r, Fold and keep us in thy care;

May our ²eyes thy law be-hold, Pur-er far than pur-est gold;
May they nev-er wea-ry be, But with ⁸gladness fol-low thee:
With the an-gels, by and by, Up ¹³a-bove the star-ry sky:

May our ²eyes thy law be-hold, Pur-er far than pur-est gold.

May our ³ears de-light to hear All ⁴thy words of love so dear;
Guard our ⁹hearts and lips from wrong, Lead us gent-ly all day long;
Oh, how ¹⁴hap-py we shall be When ¹⁵thy bless-ed face we see;

May our ⁵hands their work ful-fil, Sowing ⁶seeds of kindness still.
Tune our ¹⁰tongues, that we may sing Grateful ¹¹praise to thee our King.
When ¹⁶our gold-en sheaves we bring, And thy praise for ev-er sing.

Copyright, 1896, by Jno R. Sweney.

MOTIONS.—1, Hands together in the attitude of prayer. 2, Eyes uplifted. 3, Pointing to the ears. 4, Looking upward at the word thy. 5, Both hands held out. 6, Right hand moving to and fro. 7, Looking down at the feet. 8, Eyes uplifted. 9, Right hand on the heart, forefinger of the left pointing to the lips. 10, Pointing to the mouth. 11, Eyes uplifted. 12, Hand on the breast at the word we, and eyes uplifted at the word thee. 13, Pointing upward. 14, Turning to each other. 15, Pointing upward. 16, Arms outstretched as though clasping a bundle.

Little Daisies Nodding.

E. E. Hewitt.
Jno. R. Sweney.

1. Little daisies ¹nodding In the dewy ²grass, Smile a gentle welcome
2. Little bees ⁶a-flut-ter, Thro' the sunny hours, Gathering the hon-ey
3. See the ⁵snowy blossoms, ⁹Swinging in the breeze, They will grow to fruitage

Un-to all who ³pass, Let us be as cheer-y, And as bright as²they,
From the fragrant ²flow'rs: Let us be as bus-y, There is work for all;
On the autumn ⁸trees: So let us be ¹⁰growing In our Saviour's love;

D. S.—Let us be as cheer-y, Sing, and work a-way,

Fine. CHORUS.

For the loving ⁴Fath-er, Keeps us all the day. Trusting, trusting
Jesus needs the ⁷children, Let us heed his call.
Blessed fruit will rip-en, For the ⁴land a-bove.

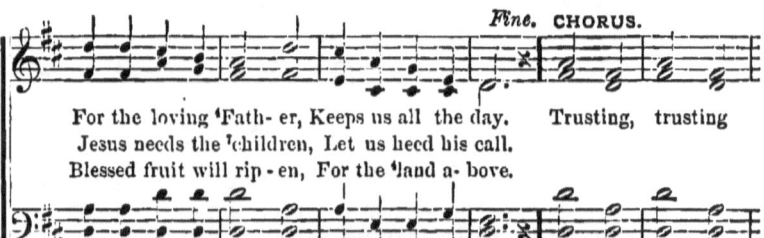

For the loving ⁴Fath-er, Keeps us all the day.

D. S.

All the happy day; Sing-ing, sing-ing, Like the birds of May,

Copyright, 1896, by Jno R. Sweney.

Motions.—1, Nod heads. 2, Point down. 3, Step forward and back. 4, Point up. 5, Hands wafted upward. 6, Move hands about. 7, Point to self. 8, Point as if to a tree. 9, Swing uplifted hand. 10, Lift both arms gradually, as high as possible. Let the teacher, facing the children, lead them in the motions, as they sing.

A TALK ABOUT TREES.

WHAT do we see in this picture?
Yes, a tree.
There is a verse in the first Psalm which speaks of the tree. Can you say it?
He shall be like a tree planted by the rivers of water, that bringeth forth his fruit in his season; his leaf also shall not wither, and whatsoever he doeth shall prosper.
Yes, the Bible says a Christian is like— Like what?
Let us see how this is
A tree, first of all, must be planted; so to be a Christian we must give up ourselves to the Lord Jesus; this is what the Bible calls being rooted in him, or rooted in love.
Then after a tree is planted and sends out its little roots under ground—It does what? Yes, it begins to grow upward, so when we love Jesus we grow in all right things.
The trees put forth?—Leaves. Yes, leaves that rustle, and make music when the winds blow upon them; so we must have leaves of praise to rustle into song when the Holy Spirit breathes upon them.
This tree in our verse has something else—Fruit.
Another Bible verse. What kind of fruit God expects his little trees to bear for him, and we will learn it, and then ask him to make this fruit grow in us.
The fruit of the spirit is love, joy, peace, longsuffering, gentleness, goodness, faith, meekness, temperance. —E. E. H.

94. Happy in a Saviour's Love.

Henrietta E. Blair. — Wm. J. Kirkpatrick.

1. While we walk by faith in the King's highway, Happy in a Saviour's love;
2. Tho' the clouds may form and the storms may fall, Happy in a Saviour's love;
3. O the peace that dwells in a trusting soul, Happy in a Saviour's love;
4. We are going home from a world of care, Happy in a Saviour's love;

We will work and sing, we will watch and pray, Happy in a Saviour's love.
With a firm, strong hope we may leave them all, Happy in a Saviour's love.
We can shout for joy, tho' the waves may roll, Happy in a Saviour's love.
By the grace of God we shall soon be there, Happy in a Saviour's love.

CHORUS.

In a Sa - - viour's love, In a Sa - - - viour's love;
In a Saviour's love, In a Saviour's love, Happy in a Saviour's love;
We will work and sing, we will watch and pray, Happy in a Saviour's love.

Copyright, 1892, by Wm. J. Kirkpatrick.

On, Little Pilgrims.

E. E. Hewitt.   Jno. R. Sweney.

1. On, little pilgrims, the Lord is King! Serving him faithfully, gladly sing;
2. Let us remember, when foes we meet, Jesus is watching the little feet;
3. On, little pilgrims, now bravely on! "Looking to Jesus," our crowns are won;

Walk after him in the ways of love, Happy the footsteps that lead above.
Trusting, obeying, we need not stray, He will take care of us all the way.
Crowns to lay down at the Saviour's feet, When by his grace at the throne we meet.

CHORUS.

March, march along, with a joyful song; Under his banner we march along;
March, march along, with a song of praise, Follow the Master in his ways.

Copyright, 1895, by Jno. R. Sweney.

A METHOD OF TEACHING THE BOOKS OF THE BIBLE.

'Have two charts of white holland, one for the Old Testament, one for the New. On these charts are lines for shelves, a shelf for each class of books; and on each shelf, pictures of the books that belong to that class, with the name of the book painted thereon. Make the books of the different classes of contrasting colors, thus the Law books, brown, the History books, crimson, etc.
—E. E. H.

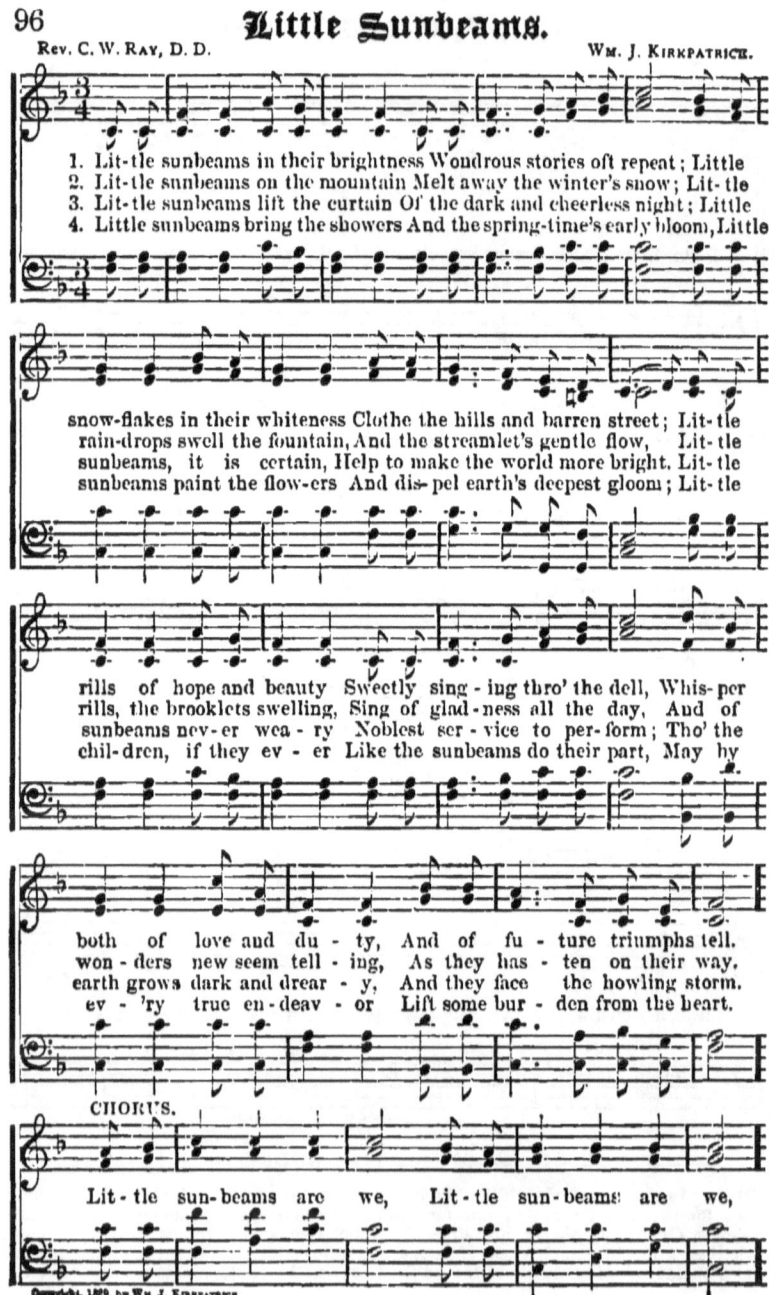

Little Sunbeams.—CONCLUDED.

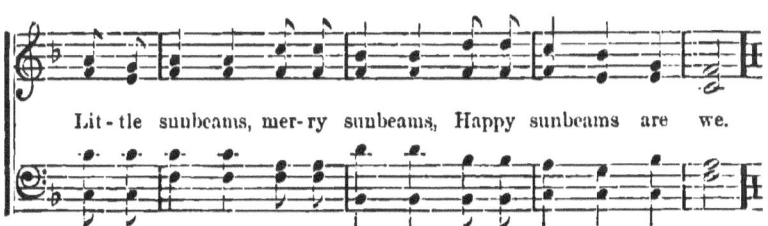

Lit-tle sunbeams, mer-ry sunbeams, Happy sunbeams are we.

Soft on the Winter Air.

ELIZA M. SHERMAN. J. E. HALL.
Joyfully. 

1. Soft on the winter air Joy-bells are ringing, Sweetly the
2. "Je-sus was born for you," Sweet is the sto-ry; Crown him with
3. Lil-ies so pure and white, Bending so low-ly, Send heav'nward

CHORUS.

Christmas tide Children are singing. Je-sus is born to-day,
love and trust, Crown him with glo-ry.
incense sweet To Christ the ho-ly.

Sweetly the children say; O give him love and praise, Thro' these glad days.

Copyright, 1880 by John J. Hood.

Two Builders.

E. E. Hewitt.
Wm. J. Kirkpatrick.

1. Two builders are at work to-day, We hear the blessed Master say,
2. One builds upon the living Rock: He need not fear the tempest-shock;
3. The other builds upon the sand: He does not heed the Lord's command;
4. Is Jesus our Foundation-Stone? And do we rest on him alone?

Up-on the rock, upon the sand; One house shall fall, and one shall stand.
His hope in Jesus is secure, His house forever shall endure.
The rain will fall, the winds will blow; His house they soon will overthrow.
Then golden service let us bring, And love's bright jewels, for our King.

CHORUS.

Build - ing, ev - 'ry one, Building till the work of life is done;
Building, building,

Build - ing; Lord, we pray, Help us to build on thee each day.
Building, we are building;

Copyright, 1904, by Wm. J. Kirkpatrick.

Jesus the Children's Friend.

W. L. M. W. L. Mason.

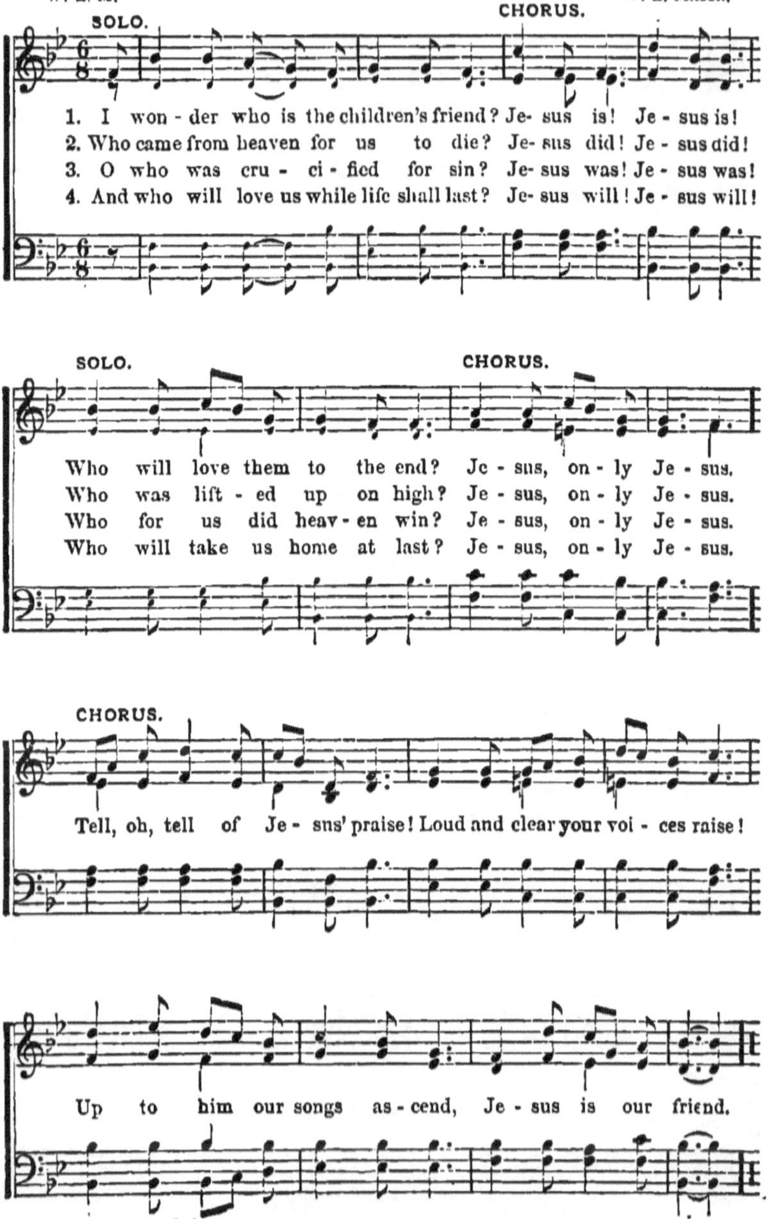
SOLO.
CHORUS.
1. I won - der who is the children's friend? Je- sus is! Je - sus is!
2. Who came from heaven for us to die? Je- sus did! Je - sus did!
3. O who was cru - ci - fied for sin? Je- sus was! Je - sus was!
4. And who will love us while life shall last? Je- sus will! Je - sus will!
SOLO.
CHORUS.
Who will love them to the end? Je - sus, on - ly Je - sus.
Who was lift - ed up on high? Je - sus, on - ly Je - sus.
Who for us did heav - en win? Je - sus, on - ly Je - sus.
Who will take us home at last? Je - sus, on - ly Je - sus.
CHORUS.
Tell, oh, tell of Je - sus' praise! Loud and clear your voi - ces raise!
Up to him our songs as - cend, Je - sus is our friend.

Loving Each Other.

101

D. E. L.   "Let us love one another."—1 John iv : 1.   D. E. Lorenz. By per.

1. This is the motto we all would obey, We will all love one anoth - er;
2. Thus will we labor and thus will we play, Trying to help one anoth - er;
3. Let us, like Jesus, be thoughtful and kind, Striving to please one another;

Happy we sing and are glad all the day, When we can serve one anoth- er.
Driving the sorrows of others away, Bringing sweet peace to each other.
Here, as in heav'n, we will be of one mind, Ev'ry one loving the oth - er.

CHORUS.

Lov- - - ing each oth - er, How pleasant to cherish a brother;
Loving and serving each oth - er,

Serv - - ing each oth - er, The Saviour looks on us with joy.
Serving and lov - ing each oth - er,

Copyright, 1885, by E. S. Lorenz.

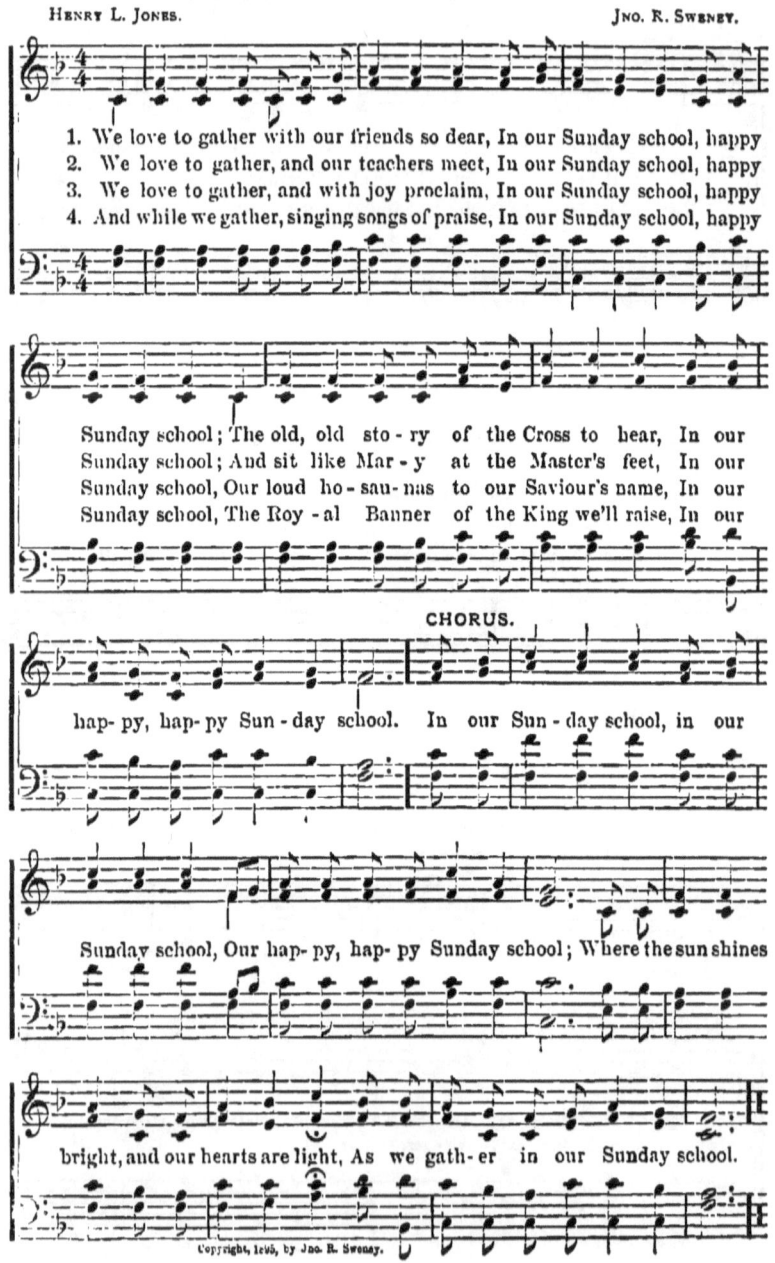

Words of Jesus.

E. E. Hewitt. Wm. J. Kirkpatrick.

Matt. xi. 28. 1. Come unto me, the Saviour said, Come unto me, the Saviour said;
John xiv. 6. 2. I am the way, the truth, the life, I am the way, the truth, the life;
Mark x. 21. 3. Take up the cross, and follow me, Take up the cross, and follow me;
Matt. vii. 7. 4. Ask and it shall be given you, Ask and it shall be given you;

Come unto me, the Saviour said, And I will give you rest.
I am the way, the truth, the life, I am the light of the world. John viii. 12.
Take up the cross, and fol-low me, And thou shalt have treasure in heaven.
Ask and it shall be giv-en you, Seek and ye shall find.

CHORUS.

Oh, the blessed words of Je - sus! Precious words! hallowed words!

Oh, the blessed words of Je - sus! Words of life to me.

John iii. 36.
5 He that believeth | on the Son, :||
Hath everlasting | life.

Is. xlv. 22.
6 Look unto me, and | be ye saved, :||
All the ends of the | earth.

Matt. v. 8.
7 Blessed are the | pure in heart, :||
For | they shall see | God.

Matt v. 12.
8 Re- | joice and be ex- | ceeding glad, :"
For | great is your reward in | heaven.

John xiv. 18.
9 I | will not leave you | comfortless, ||
I will come unto | you.

John vii. 37.
10 If | any man thirst let him | come unto
And drink of the water of | life. [me, :||

Mark. x. 14.
11 Suffer little children to | come unto
me. :|| [heaven.
For of | such is the kingdom of |

John xiv. 2.
12 I | go to prepare a | place for you, ||
In my Fathers' house.

Copyright, 1888, by Wm. J. Kirkpatrick.

Spring Emblems. 105

[*A song-exercise for five little girls. Let the children carry bouquets, baskets, wreaths of spring flowers, or sprays of green.*]

E. E. Hewitt.   Wm. J. Kirkpatrick.

1st.- Beneath the cov-er-lid of snow The sleeping blossoms lay,
2nd.- The emerald grass bedecks the way With carpets fresh and fair;
3rd.- The lit-tle streamlets gladly run, With laughter in their flow,
4th.- The birds return to us a-gain, From south-lands far a-way,
5th.- So na-ture tells the sto-ry sweet, That winter yields to spring;

But woke to beau-ty in the glow Of springtime's gentle ray.
The trees put on their green ar-ray, Be-cause new life is there.
And, sparkling in the gold-en sun, On hap-py errands go.
And war-ble in each joy-ous strain God's praises all the day.
Her lips the bless-ed news re-peat, And hail our Je-sus King.

CHORUS, by the five.

Bloom, lovely flow'rs, In spring's bright hours, While earth with music rings;

Our songs of praise To Christ we raise, Im-mor-tal life he brings.

Copyright, 1893, by Wm. J. Kirkpatrick.

Story of the Autumn Leaves. 107

E. E. HEWITT.   JNO. R. SWENEY.

1. Fresh young leaves upon the trees Fluttered in the play-ful breeze,
2. Un-der sun-ny skies of blue Budding leaves much larger grew,
3. Autumn days have come a-gain, Pluck the fruit and cut the grain;

Made a plea-sant, pret-ty home, Where the lit-tle birds could come.
From the heat a shel-ter made By their green and cool-ing shade;
Fall-ing leaves of red and gold Have their year-ly les-sons told.

Build a snug and cunning nest, Sing the songs they love the best. Falling, falling,
Moving gently to and fro When the summer winds breathed low. Falling, falling,
Serve the Lord, glad hearts and free, Beautiful all life will be. Falling, falling,

fall - ing; Fallen leaves upon the grass Say the days of spring must pass.
fall - - ing; Fallen leaves upon the grass Say the summer glories pass.
fall - - ing; Fallen leaves upon the grass; To an endless spring must pass.

FIRST VERSE, 1st, 2d, and 3d lines—Arms upraised with fluttering fingers; 4th—Flight motion of hands upward; 5th and 6th—Hands together, nest shape; 7th—Arms raised, gently lowered at each "falling"; 8th and 9th—Pointing down. SECOND VERSE, 1st, 2d, and 3d—Arms upraised, fingers meeting overhead; 4th—Arms raised, hands spread out branch-wise; 5th and 6th—Gentle fluttering of fingers; 7th—Arms raised, gently lowered at each "falling"; 8th and 9th—Pointing down. THIRD VERSE, 2d line—Motion of plucking fruit with right hands; scythe motion; 3d-7th—Arms raised, gently lowered at each "falling"; 9th—Hands placed together as in praise, look upward.

THE USE OF THE BIBLE.

How must we handle the Bible?
With care and reverence.
If we can read, how often must we read the Bible?
Every day.
How must we read it?
With prayer, that we may understand it.
Is it enough to read the Word of God?
No, we must love it, remember its teachings and try to do them.
What does David say about loving the Bible?
"Thy word have I hid in mine heart, that I might not sin against thee."
What is said about remembering the words we read?
"Remember his commandments to do them."
What did the Lord Jesus say about keeping his words? (Recite with motions.)
Whosoever heareth these sayings of mine, and doeth them, I will liken him unto a wise man, which built his house upon a rock: and the rain descended, and the floods came, and the winds blew, and beat upon that house; and it fell not: for it was founded upon a rock. —E. E. H

110. Temperance Pledge Song.

E. E. Hewitt.   Jno. R. Sweney.

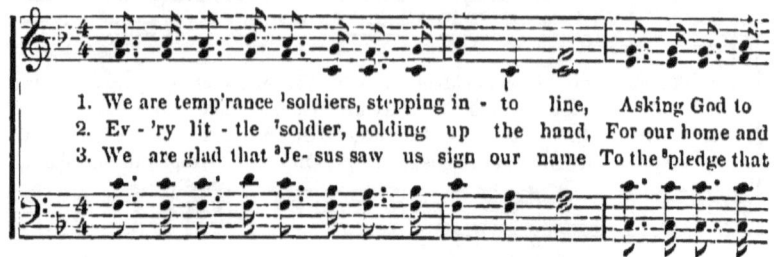

1. We are temp'rance ¹soldiers, stepping in-to line, Asking God to
2. Ev-'ry lit-tle ²soldier, holding up the hand, For our home and
3. We are glad that ³Je-sus saw us sign our name To the ⁸pledge that

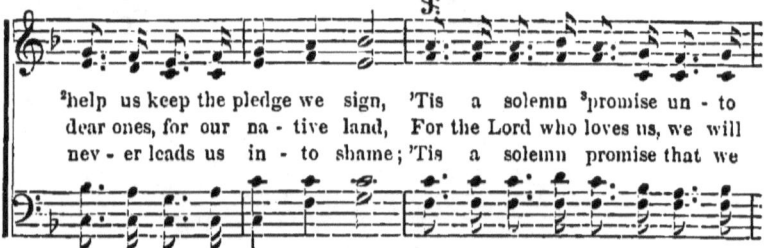

²help us keep the pledge we sign, 'Tis a solemn ³promise un-to
dear ones, for our na-tive land, For the Lord who loves us, we will
nev-er leads us in-to shame; 'Tis a solemn promise that we

D. S.—Save our land for ⁶Je-sus, from the

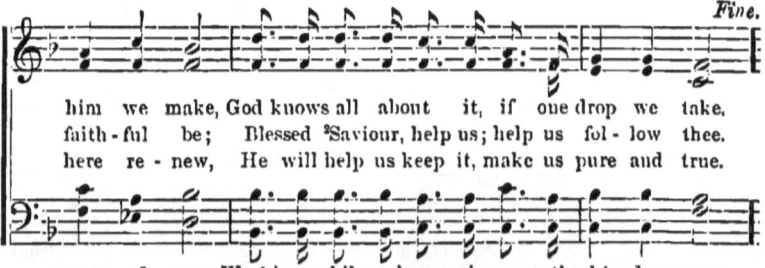

him we make, God knows all about it, if one drop we take.
faith-ful be; Blessed ⁷Saviour, help us; help us fol-low thee.
here re-new, He will help us keep it, make us pure and true.

power of rum, Working, while we're praying may thy kingdom come.

CHORUS.   D. S.

[stand;
Forward! ⁴forward! we're a temp'rance band, Forward! forward! ⁵bravely let us

Copyright, 1886, by Jno. R. Sweney.

MOTIONS.—1, Keep step. 2, Clasp hands, bow head. 3, Point up. 4, Join hands, keep step. 5, Bring down right foot, firmly. 6, Wave arm, as if waving flag. 7, Hold up right hand. 8, Motion of writing.

Feathers and Fur.

E. E. Hewitt.   (For Bands of Mercy.)   Clarissa H. Spencer.

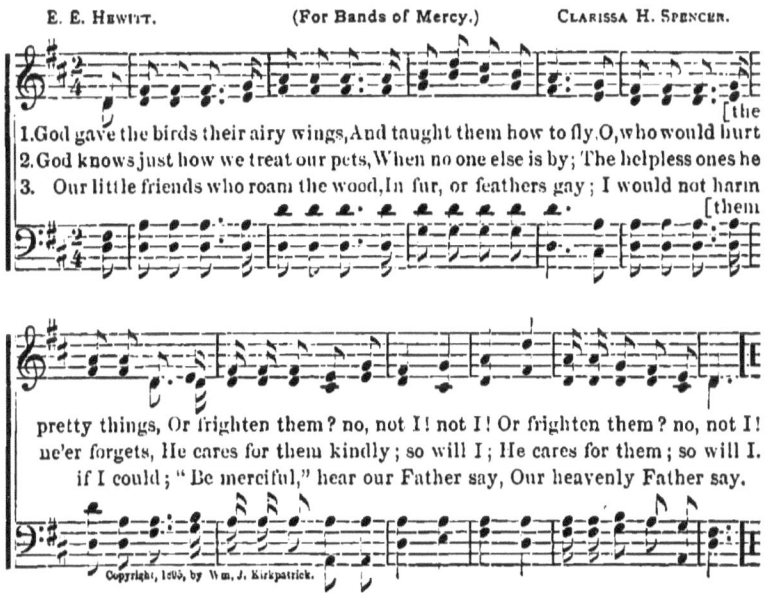

1. God gave the birds their airy wings, And taught them how to fly. O, who would hurt [the
2. God knows just how we treat our pets, When no one else is by; The helpless ones he
3. Our little friends who roam the wood, In fur, or feathers gay; I would not harm [them

pretty things, Or frighten them? no, not I! not I! Or frighten them? no, not I!
ne'er forgets, He cares for them kindly; so will I; He cares for them; so will I.
if I could; "Be merciful," hear our Father say, Our heavenly Father say.

Copyright, 1895, by Wm. J. Kirkpatrick.

TEMPERANCE.

What is a temperance pledge?
A solemn promise never to use intoxicating drinks.
Ought any one to take such a pledge without understanding it?
No; we must know what it means.
Should we take such a pledge without prayer?
No, we need God's help to keep it.
What are intoxicating drinks?
Drinks which may lead to drunkenness.
What drinks will lead to drunkenness?
Those which contain alcohol.
What is alcohol?
Alcohol is a poison.
Name some drinks which contain alcohol?
Ale, beer, cider, wine, whiskey, gin, brandy.
Why is it sinful to take such drinks?
Because it is sinful to hurt our bodies or souls.
Does alcohol do this?
Yes; alcohol injures both body and soul.
Should we eat pudding sauces, pies or candy, flavored with liquor?
We should not.
Why not?
Because it is the nature of alcohol to give us a taste to wish for more.

What damage is there in just a little?
One taste may lead to another till a dreadful habit is formed.
What is the only safe way?
Touch not, taste not, handle not.
Sing. "Temperance Pledge Song." on opposite page.
"Who hath woe? who hath sorrow? who hath contentions? who hath babbling? who hath wounds without cause? who hath redness of eyes?"
"They that tarry long at the wine; they that go to seek mixed wine."
What does God tell us?
"Look not thou upon the wine when it is red, when it giveth his color in the cup, when it moveth itself aright. At the last it biteth like a serpent, and stingeth like an adder."
Is it sinful to give these drinks to others if we do not use them ourselves?
God says, Wo unto him that giveth his neighbor drink."
Can any drunkard enter into the beautiful home above?
No; God says, "There shall in no wise enter into it anything that defileth."
What good rule does God give us?
Whether therefore ye eat or drink, or whatsoever ye do, do all to the glory of God.

The Door of My Lips. 113

RECITE.—Let the words of my mouth, and the meditation of my heart, be acceptable in thy sight, O Lord, my strength, and my Redeemer. Ps. xix: 14. For there is not a word in my tongue, but, lo, O Lord, thou knowest it altogether. Ps. cxxxix: 4.

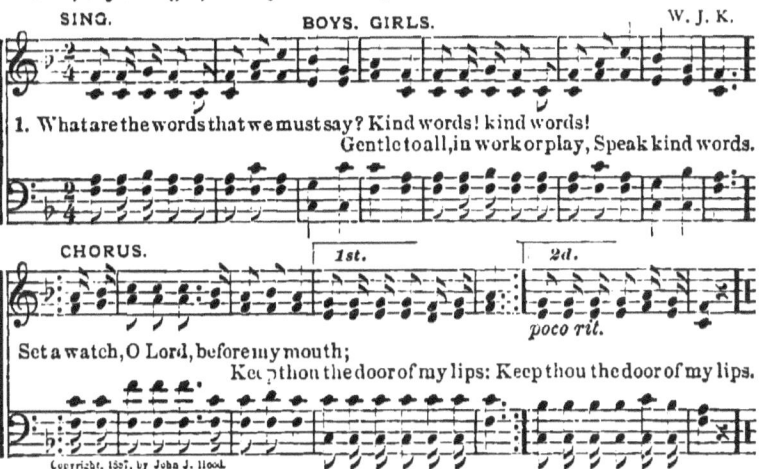

SING. BOYS. GIRLS. W. J. K.

1. What are the words that we must say? Kind words! kind words! Gentle to all, in work or play, Speak kind words.

CHORUS. 1st. 2d. poco rit.

Set a watch, O Lord, before my mouth; Keep thou the door of my lips: Keep thou the door of my lips.

Copyright, 1887, by John J. Hood.

RECITE.—A soft answer turneth away wrath, but grievous words stir up anger. Prov. xv: 1.

2 What are the words that we must say?
ABr True words! true words!
God's own command we must obey,
Speak true words.

CHO.—Set a watch, O Lord, before my Keep thou the door of my lips.:‖[mouth;

RECITE.—The ninth commandment is, "Thou shalt not bear false witness against thy neighbor." Ex. xx: 16. Lying lips are abomination to the Lord, but they that deal truly are his delight. Prov. xii: 22.

3 What are the words that we must say?
Pure words! pure words!
Pure as the shining light of day;
Speak pure words.

CHO.—Set a watch, O Lord, before my Keep thou the door of my lips.:‖[mouth;

RECITE.—The third commandment is, "Thou shalt not take the name of the Lord thy God in vain: for the Lord will not hold him guiltless that taketh his name in vain." Ex. xx: 7 Let no corrupt communication proceed out of your mouth. Eph. iv: 29.

4 What are the words that we must say?
Bright words! bright words!
Happy of heart as birds in May;
Speak bright words.

CHO.—Set a watch, O Lord, before my Keep thou the door of my lips.:‖[mouth;

RECITE.—Pleasant words are as a honeycomb, sweet to the soul. Prov. xvi: 24. A word spoken in due season, how good is it. Prov. xv: 23.

5 What are the words that we must say?
Good words! good words!
Loving the Lord, we'll sing and pray;
Speak good words.

CHO.—Set a watch, O Lord, before my Keep thou the door of my lips.:‖[mouth;

RECITE.—It is a good thing to give thanks unto the Lord, and to sing praise unto thy name, O most high. Ps. xcii: 1 Continue in prayer. Col. iv: 2. And whatsoever ye do, in word or deed, do all in the name of the Lord Jesus. Col. iii: 17.

CHO.—Set a watch, O Lord, before my Keep thou the door of my lips.:‖[mouth;
—E. E. Hewitt.

A PLEDGE.

God help me evermore to keep
 This promise that I make,—
I will not swear, nor smoke, nor chew,
 Nor pois'nous liquors take;

I'll try to get my little friends
 To make this promise too,
And every day I'll try to find
 Some helpful work to do.
—Selected.

How Do the Woods.

(May be adapted for Children's Day by altering the words Easter Day as required.)
(A motion-song for selected children.)

E. E. Hewitt.   Wm. J. Kirkpatrick.

1. How do the woods keep Easter Day? With ¹waving boughs, like banners gay,
2. How do the flow'rs keep Easter Day? They ³peep above the ground, this way,
3. How do the birds keep Easter Day? Up ⁵from the south, they find the way,
4. How do the lambs keep Easter Day? Up-on the ⁷hills they skip and play;
5. How do the children keep the day? They sing their hymns, they ¹³humbly pray;

And lit-tle ²leaves on all the trees, A-flutter³ in the pleasant breeze.
While sunbeams shine, and ⁴raindrops fall, They give ⁵their sweetness out to all.
They ⁹build their lit-tle nests, and sing The merry carols of the spring.
They do not know, as ¹¹we all do About our ¹²Shepherd, good and true.
And ev-'ry heart ¹⁴sweet praises gives, So ¹⁵glad, so ¹⁶glad, for Jesus lives.

Sweet Easter Day, bright Easter Day, The woods ¹hang out their banners gay;
Sweet Easter Day, bright Easter Day, Beneath the ⁶ground, the seedlet lay,
Sweet Easter Day, bright Easter Day, They ⁸spread their wings, and fly away;
Sweet Easter Day, bright Easter Day, Because ¹⁰they know no better way,
Sweet Easter Day, bright Easter Day, The children ¹³bow their heads and pray;

Copyright, 1894, by Wm. J. Kirkpatrick.

How do the Woods.—CONCLUDED.

DUET OR SEMI-CHORUS.   **CHORUS.**

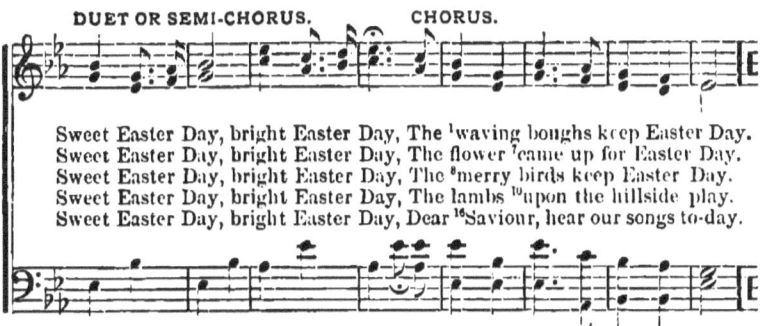

Sweet Easter Day, bright Easter Day, The ¹waving boughs keep Easter Day.
Sweet Easter Day, bright Easter Day, The flower ⁷came up for Easter Day.
Sweet Easter Day, bright Easter Day, The ⁸merry birds keep Easter Day.
Sweet Easter Day, bright Easter Day, The lambs ¹⁰upon the hillside play.
Sweet Easter Day, bright Easter Day, Dear ¹⁶Saviour, hear our songs to-day.

MOTIONS.—1, Arms waved above heads. 2, Arms raised with fluttering fingers. 3, Sink down, and slowly rise. 4, With fingers of right hand strike the palm of left. 5, Waving motion, outward. 6, Point to ground. 7, Slowly raise hands. 8, Flight motion. 9, Hands together like nest. 10, Skipping motion. 11, Point to self. 12, Point up. 13, Bow heads, and clasp hands. 14, Hands pressed against left side. 15, Lightly clap hands. 16, Arms thrown upward.

Rose-bud Song.

F. G. Burroughs.   Jno. R. Sweney.
Andante.

1. I am on-ly a lit-tle rose-bud, Scarcely a-ble to be seen,
2. Though I am but a ti-ny rose-bud, Yet I have a work to do;
3. God has given me form and col-or, He has put me here to bloom;
4. Brief may be my days of fragrance, Yet my mis-sion I'll ful-fil,

But my pe-tals soon will o-pen And un-fold my ca-lyx green.
I can hon-or my dear Mak-er, Praising him as well as you.
And he bids me cheer his chil-dren By my soft and sweet perfume.
For I know that e'en a rose-bud Can o-bey its Maker's will.

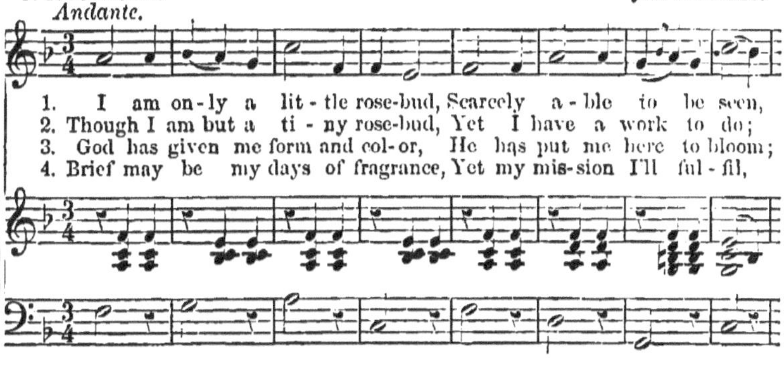

Copyright, 1881, 1886, by John J. Hood.

116. Three Cheers for the Flag.

E. E. Hewitt.   Jno. R. Sweney.

1. Our banner to the breezes fling, Three cheers for the flag we love; The boys and girls will shout and sing, Three cheers for the flag we love. Hurrah! hurrah! hurrah! [Three cheers for the flag we love; Hurrah! hurrah! hurrah! Three cheers for the flag we love.
2. 'Twas for this flag our fathers fought, Three cheers for the flag we love; Their blood our country's freedom bought, Three cheers for the flag we love.
3. We'll stand for all that's pure and right, Three cheers for the flag we love; In goodness is a nation's might, Three cheers for the flag we love.
4. May peace and plenty crown our land, Three cheers for the flag we love; And may we know God's guiding hand, Three cheers for the flag we love.

CHORUS.

Copyright, 1895, by Jno. R. Sweney.

117. When Jesus was a Child.

E. E. Hewitt.   Jno. R. Sweney.

1. When Jesus was a little child His life was pure and true, And
2. Around the hills of Nazareth, He played, as boys delight; He
3. He made his earthly parents glad, By loving, helpful ways, No
4. He loved his heavenly Father's house, The temple of the Lord; With

Copyright, 1892, by Jno. R. Sweney.

When Jesus, etc.—CONCLUDED.

as he gained in years, he grew In grace and wisdom too.
loved the lilies of the field, And watched the song-bird's flight.
selfish word nor angry look Stained those sweet childhood days.
psalm and precept, Bible words, His memory was stored.

D.S.—pray sincerely for his help, His own dear child to be.

CHORUS.

How glad I am, my Saviour once Was a little child like me, I'll

118. The Little Vine.

E. E. Hewitt.   Wm. J. Kirkpatrick.

1. In a sunny corner, Grows a little vine, And its little tendrils
2. So would I be growing, Like the little vine, Climbing up to heaven,

CHORUS.

'Round the arbor twine. Growing, growing, In the sunshine gay,
Where the sunbeams shine.

Higher, higher, Climbing ev'ry day.

3 All the sweet heart-tendrils
Must to Jesus cling,
Trusting, while I serve him,
Trusting, while I cling.

4 Then some fruit for Jesus,
In my life I'll bear,
Faith, and hope, and patience,
Loving deeds, and prayer.

Copyright, 1896, by Wm. J. Kirkpatrick.

119. Tender Saviour.

E. E. Hewitt. Wm. J. Kirkpatrick.

1. Tender Saviour, by whose childhood Ev-'ry little child is blest,
2. Hold us by thy hand, dear Saviour, Lead us in thy ho-ly ways;
3. Walking in thy gen-tle footsteps, Help us, Lord, to follow thee;
4. Make our childhood bright with sunshine, Keep us by thy favor blest,

Help us love and trust and serve thee, Fold us to thy gen-tle breast.
Growing in thy grace and wisdom, Fill our hearts with joyful praise.
Make us pure and true and lov-ing, Make us more and more like thee.
And when earthly life is o-ver Fold us to thy gen-tle breast.

Ten-der Saviour, lov-ing Saviour, Fold us to thy gen-tle breast.
Ten-der Saviour, lov-ing Saviour, Fill our hearts with joyful praise.
Ten-der Saviour, lov-ing Saviour, Make us more and more like thee.
Ten-der Saviour, lov-ing Saviour, Fold us to thy gen-tle breast.

Copyright, 1892, by Wm. J. Kirkpatrick.

120. Children of Zion.

Mrs. E. C. Ellsworth. Chas. Edw. Prior.

DUET. *Cheerfully.*

1. Oh, many, many children In Zion shall be found; We hear their happy
2. Oh, who will be the children Within the city bright? Will you be one to
3. Then come and bring a playmate, Perchance a brother dear; Let sisters come to-

voi-ces, And pleasant is the sound; For children can be Christians, And
en-ter, And come by morning light? Oh, do not wait till old-er— The
geth-er. Oh, nev-er, nev-er fear; For Zi-on must have children Up-

Copyright, 1885, by John J. Hood.

Countless are the Blessings.—CONCLUDED.

CHORUS.

Or the grains of sand. Cheerfully, cheerfully let us give, Cheerfully, cheerfully,
All the joys we share.
Half the debt we owe.
Bless the gifts they bring.

ev - er, Cheerfully, cheerfully let us give, God loveth a cheerful giv- er.

124 Jewels for the Master.

FANNY J. CROSBY.   WM. J. KIRKPATRICK.
not too fast.

1. Jewels for the Master, Oh, how glad are we; Jewels for his kingdom
2. Jewels for the Master, Precious in his sight; May his Spirit keep us

CHORUS.

Lit- tle ones may be.   Jewels he is watching With a tender love;
Ev - er pure and bright.

By and by to sparkle In his crown above.

3 Jewels, costly jewels,
Purchased not with gold;
But the price that bought us
Never can be told.

4 Jewels for the Master,
From his mansions fair
May not one be missing;
May we all be there.

Copyright, 1895, by Wm. J. Kirkpatrick.

125. The Little Gleaner.

J. J. Lowa.

1. I am a lit-tle gleaner, Among the harvest sheaves; I follow in the reaping, For what the reaper leaves: For hap-ly by the wayside Some handfuls may be tossed, As said the careful Master, That nothing shall be lost.
2. Drops fill the boundless ocean, Sands pile the mountain high; So all the bounteous garner Must single grains supply. And when to feed the hungry The richer off'ring comes, The full loaf on the ta-ble May not disdain the crumbs.
3. I'm sor-ry 'tis so lit-tle My little hands can do; But Jesus will ac-cept it, If but my heart is true. And sometime—'tis the promise My heart in hope believes—I'll bring the blessed Master The full and joyful sheaves.

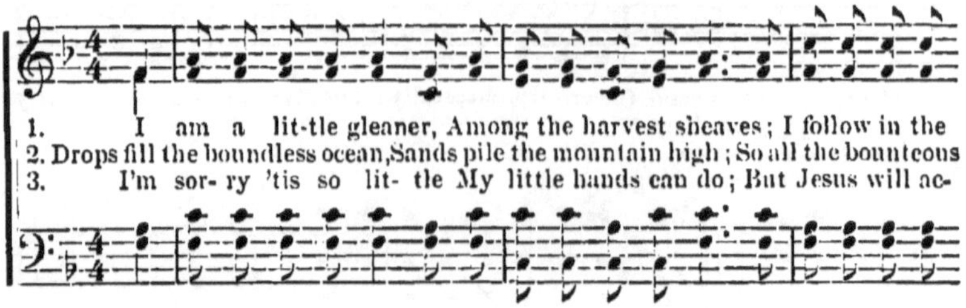

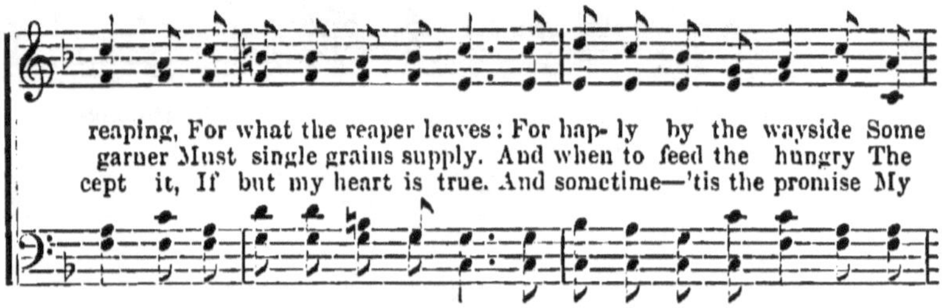

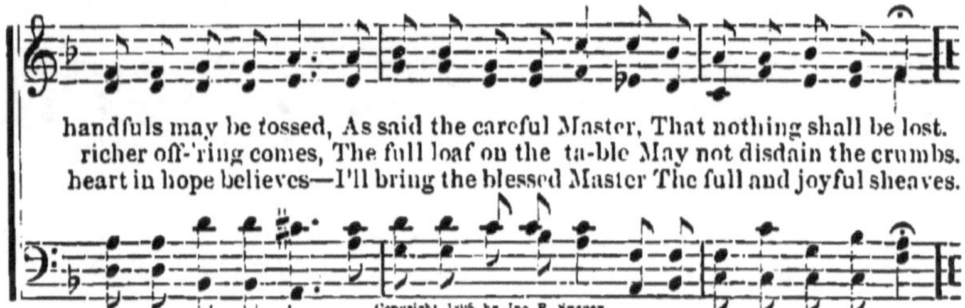

Copyright, 1895, by Jno. R. Sweney.

126. Little Bird, with Downy Breast.

"The foxes have holes, and the birds of the air have nests; but the Son of man hath not where to lay his head."—Matt. viii; 20.

E. E. Hewitt.   Wm. J. Kirkpatrick.

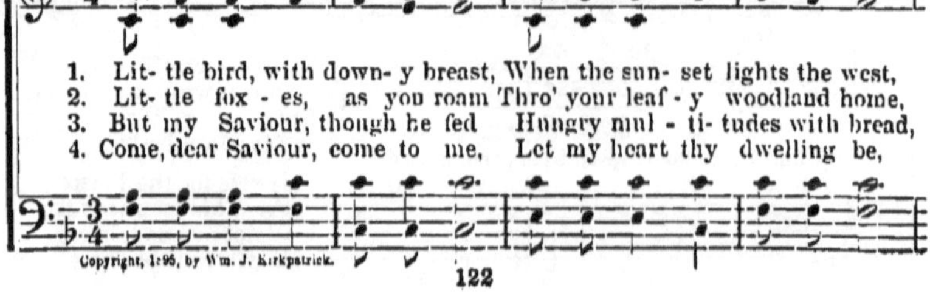

1. Lit-tle bird, with down-y breast, When the sun-set lights the west,
2. Lit-tle fox-es, as you roam Thro' your leaf-y woodland home,
3. But my Saviour, though he fed Hungry mul-ti-tudes with bread,
4. Come, dear Saviour, come to me, Let my heart thy dwelling be,

Copyright, 1895, by Wm. J. Kirkpatrick.

Little Bird, etc.—CONCLUDED.

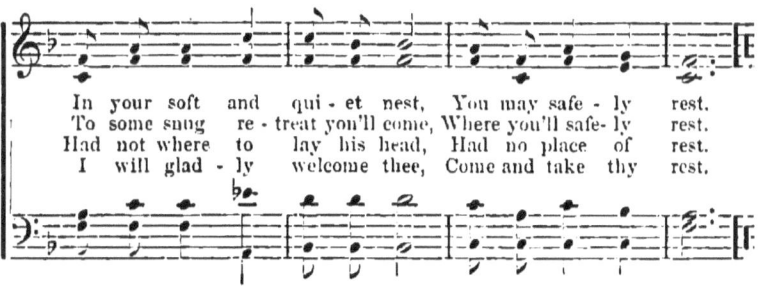

In your soft and qui-et nest, You may safe-ly rest.
To some snug re-treat you'll come, Where you'll safe-ly rest.
Had not where to lay his head, Had no place of rest.
I will glad-ly welcome thee, Come and take thy rest.

127 The Little Ones' Creed.

L. H. EDMUNDS.   WM. J. KIRKPATRICK.

1. In God my Father I believe, And trustful-ly his love receive;
2. In Christ my Saviour I believe, And joy-ful-ly his grace receive;
3. In God the Spir-it I believe, And grateful-ly his word receive;
4. In God's bright heaven I believe, Where all his children he'll receive;

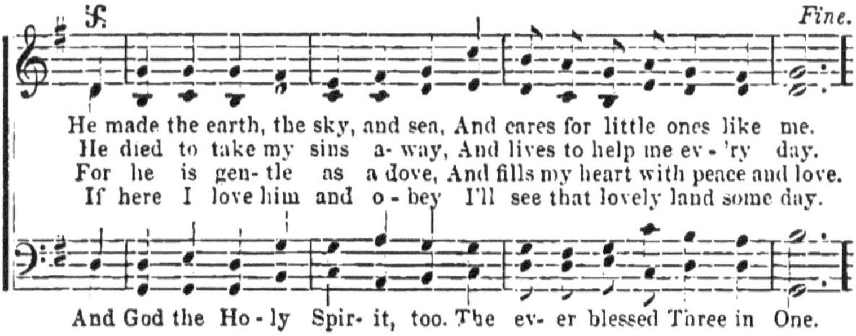

He made the earth, the sky, and sea, And cares for little ones like me.
He died to take my sins a-way, And lives to help me ev-'ry day.
For he is gen-tle as a dove, And fills my heart with peace and love.
If here I love him and o-bey I'll see that lovely land some day.

And God the Ho-ly Spir-it, too. The ev-er blessed Three in One.

CHORUS.   D.S.

I be-lieve, I be-lieve In God the Father, and the Son,
   I believe,   I believe

Copyright, 1895, by Wm J. Kirkpatrick.

Father, Bless Thy Word.—CONCLUDED.

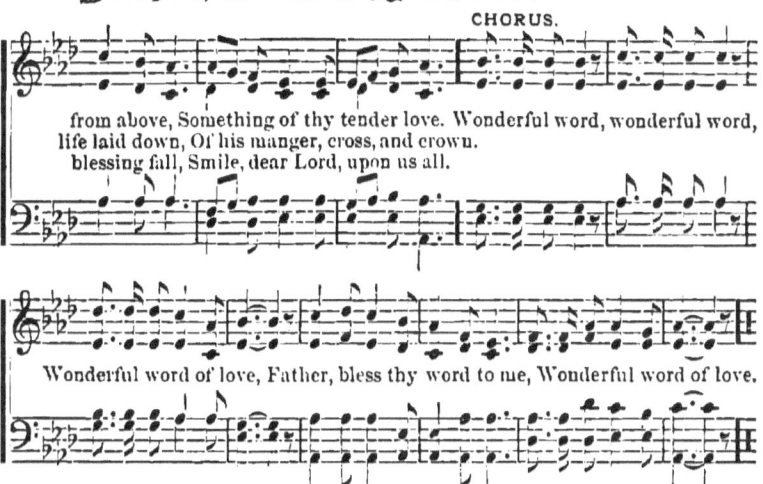

from above, Something of thy tender love. Wonderful word, wonderful word,
life laid down, Of his manger, cross, and crown.
blessing fall, Smile, dear Lord, upon us all.

Wonderful word of love, Father, bless thy word to me, Wonderful word of love.

130 I will Try to Do My Best.

E. E. Hewitt.   Wm. J. Kirkpatrick.

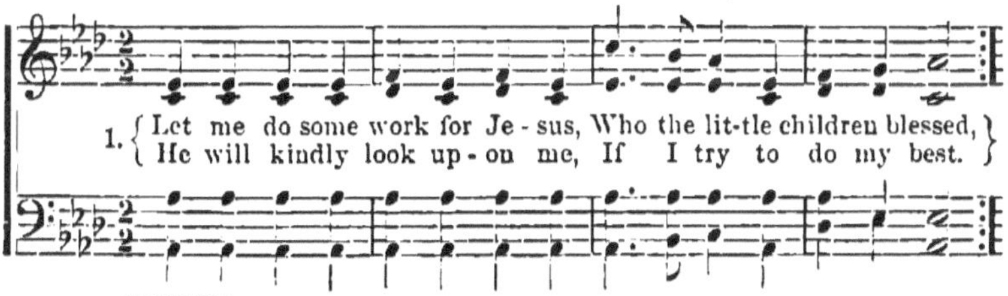

1. Let me do some work for Jesus, Who the little children blessed,
   He will kindly look upon me, If I try to do my best.

CHORUS.
I will try, I will try, I will try to do my best; Daily asking God to help me, I will try to do my best.

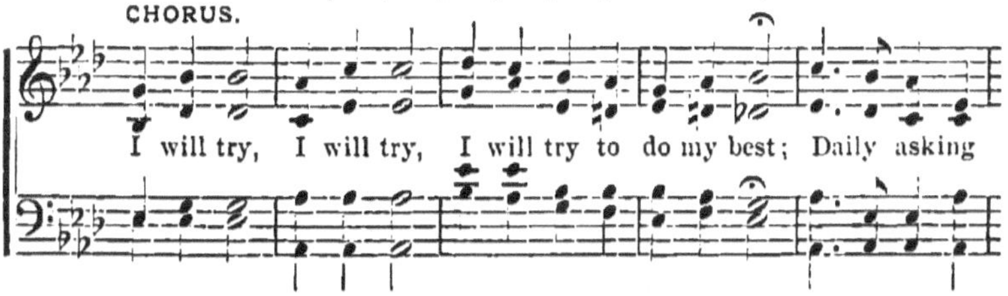

2. I have often sinned against him,
   He forgives the sin confessed;
   Now I'll trust in him to help me,
   Faithfully to do my best.

3. Jesus loves his little servants,
   In his loving arms they rest;
   Tenderly he smiles upon them,
   When they try to do their best.

131. Good By.

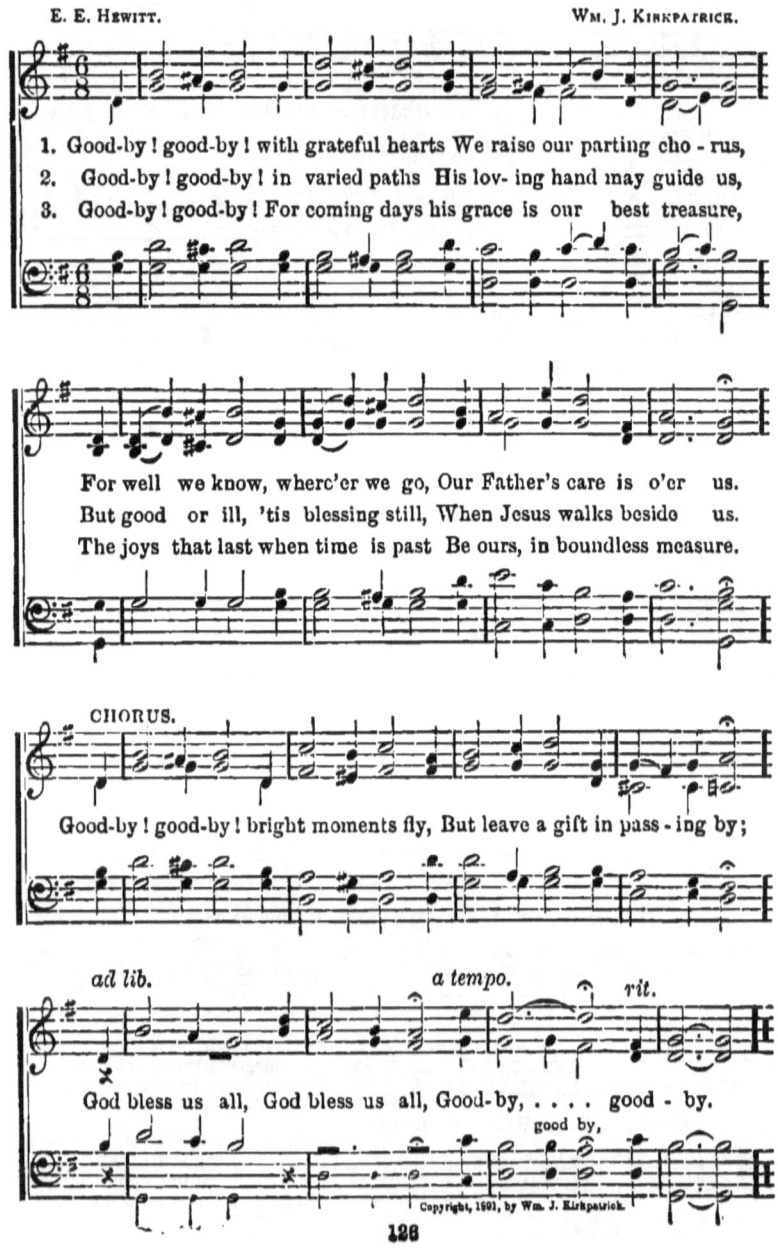

INDEX.

A certain poor widow in Zion,	59
A HAPPY LITTLE BAND,	55
A HAPPY LITTLE HOME,	14
ALL FOR JESUS,	10
ALL FOR THEE,	67
A SONG IN THE RAIN,	6
BEARING FRUIT,	44
Beneath the coverlid of snow,	105
BIRD, FLOWER, AND STAR,	75
Blossoms of the sunny spring,	3
BUILDING ON THE ROCK OF AGES,	33
Butterfly, butterfly flitting by,	91
CARRY THE LIGHT,	22
Children of Jerusalem,	88
CHILDREN OF ZION,	120
CLOSING PRAYER,	128
COME, COME, COME,	122
COME, O COME TO ME,	58
Come unto me, the Saviour said,	103
Countless are the blessings	123
Daises and buttercups, sparkling	74
Dear Father, for thy tender love,	79
DOING ITS BEST,	12
Down from the mountains,	50
EARNEST PRAYER,	71
EASTER LESSONS,	91
Father, bless thy word to me,	129
FEATHERS AND FUR,	111
Flowers breathe their fragrance	63
FOR JESUS,	121
FREELY GIVE,	8
Freely the violets sweet perfume	8
Fresh young leaves upon the trees	107
Gentle Jesus, meek and mild,	61
Gentle Shepherd, Saviour dear,	51
Gentle summer breezes, whisper-	106
GLAD HOSANNAS,	17
Glory be to Jesus,	7
God gave the birds their airy w.	111
God is in his holy temple,	5
GOD TOOK CARE OF THE BABY,	15
Good-by! good-by! with grateful	131
HALLELUJAH, AMEN,	45
HAPPY BIRTHDAYS,	40
Happy hours, happy hours,	46
HAPPY IN A SAVIOUR'S LOVE,	94
Happy little ones are we,	24
HAPPY SUNDAY SCHOOL,	102
Hear the joyful carols,	72
HEARTS OF LOVE,	28
HE CALLETH HIS SHEEP,	11
HELP US, LORD, TO LOVE THEE,	57
Help us, Lord, with every day,	57
HE SHALL FEED HIS FLOCK,	60
HIS LITTLE LAMB,	36
Holy is the Sabbath day,	87
Hosanna we sing, like the child-	16
How do the woods keep Easter d.	114
I am a little gleaner,	125
I am but a tiny cricket,	12
I am only a little rosebud,	115
If I love Jesus, the Saviour above	64
If I were a bird,	75
I know I am little,	13
I learned it in the Bible,	104
I'LL DO WHAT I CAN,	13
I'm but a child, yet Jesus died	18
In a little basket, under skies of b	15
In a precious casket,	86
In a sunny corner,	118
In God my Father I believe,	127
IN HIS TEMPLE,	5
In the days of old,	35
In the morning I will pray,	65
I think, when I read that sweet sto-	34
It was night in the temple	68
I WILL TRY TO DO MY BEST,	130
I wonder who is the children's f.	100
I would be a lily fair,	38
Jesus comes with saving grace	71
Jesus is our blessed King,	28
Jesus, my Saviour, to Bethlehem c.	52
Jesus, O thou gentle Shepherd,	47
JESUS THE CHILDREN'S FRIEND,	100
JESUS' TOUCH	9
Jewels for the Master,	124
LESSONS FROM THE CLOCK,	43
Let me do some work for Jesus,	130
LET THE BLESSED SAVIOUR IN,	81
LET THEM COME TO ME,	29
Let us ask the gracious Saviour,	80
Let us rise, let us rise,	30
Let us unite and sing his praise,	26
LIKE THE BRIGHT FLOWERS,	38
Listen! like a whispering breeze.	58
Little birds of praise are we,	27
Little bird, with downy breast,	126
LITTLE BUILDERS,	32
Little children of Jesus, we carol	90
Little daisies nodding,	92
Little feet may find the pathway,	19
LITTLE FOLKS ACROSS THE SEA,	49
LITTLE GIFTS,	48
Little hands can serve him,	83
Little hands to work for Jesus,	10
Little ones may be just like the	44
Little schoolmates, one and all,	66
Little sunbeams in their bright-	96
Little sunbeams, bright and gay,	48
LOVES YOU AND ME,	66
LOVING EACH OTHER,	101
Many in darkness are far astray,	22
MISSIONARY BAND,	82
MOTION SONG BEFORE LESSON,	30

DEW DROPS.

Murmuring stream,	50
Never alone am I.	108
Oh, come where love is bend-.	20
Oh, come with hearts rejoicing,	20
Oh, list to the brook, the bright	85
On, little pilgrims, the Lord is K.	95
Oh, many, many children,	120
O Jesus, our Shepherd,	11
Once, when a shower was falling,	6
On the bough of the tree,	14
Our banner to the breezes fling,	116
Our bible story,	109
Our dear bible verses, how bright-	31
Pleasing Jesus,	80
Praise him, every voice,	3
Praise ye the Lord, while harps of	45
Rock-a-bye, baby,.	112
Sabbath day,	87
Saviour, bless us from above,	128
Saviour, grant the children's	89
Seeking for me,	52
See our little soldier band,	55
See the little roses,	39
Shepherd, lead us,.	47
Singing his praises,	26
Sing praises, happy praises,	73
Soft on the winter air,	97
Some little work for Jesus,	42
Spring emblems,.	105
Stepping in the light,	78
Story of the autumn leaves,	107
Suffer them to come,	18
Sunday School marching song,	76
Sweet the lessons Jesus taught,	29
Swinging, gently swinging,	93
Temperance pledge song,	110
Tender Saviour, by whose child-.	119
Thankful hearts to-day we bring,.	23
The birthday box,	41
The boys and girls for Jesus,	84
The child Jesus,.	69
The children long ago, sang.	17
The children's offering,	63
The children's prayer,	89
The crown jewel,	86
The door of my lips,.	113
The golden text,	31

The heavenly Kingdom,	25
The Lambs of Jesus,	21
The little birds are singing for Je-	67
The little gleaner,	125
The little lamb in pastures fair,	86
The little lambs are frisking,	21
The little ones' creed,	127
The little vine,	118
There's a precious bible story,	109
There's a word we've often heard,	122
There stands upon the landing	43
The Sabbath bells are ringing,	4
The snow prayer,	104
The song of the brook,	85
The two mites,	59
This is the motto we all would o-.	101
Three cheers for the flag,	116
Tiny notes of music,	41
To work! said a bird from the t..	62
Trusting Jesus, 'tis the way,	33
Trying to walk in the steps of the	78
Two builders are at work to-day,.	98
Under the trees,	93
Upward, growing upward,	70
We all are little builders,	32
We are but a band of children,	82
We are coming in our gladness,	25
We are temperance soldiers,.	110
We are very glad we've heard,	49
We'll do what we can, the daisies	54
We'll give our hearts to Jesus,	37
We love to gather with our friends	102
We're marching to a land of joy.	76
We thank thee,	79
We want to live for Jesus,	121
We will sing you a beautiful story	60
What are the words that we	113
What can we do for Jesus,	99
When fades the rosy sunset light,	108
When Jesus was a little child, 69,	117
When on earth the Saviour dwelt,	9
When our pleasant birthdays come	40
While we walk by faith	94
Who stands outside the closed door	81
Words of Jesus,	103
Work for great and small,	99
Work for the children,	62

SERVICES, RESPONSIVE EXERCISES, ETC.

A bible exercise,	53
About Church going,	5
A handful of texts,	55
A method of teaching	95
An offering exercise,.	9
A pledge,	114
A talk about trees,	93
Birthday box exercise	41

Coming to Jesus,	77
Jesus loves the chil-.	67
Jesus the only Sav-	28
Lessons from the B.	66
Little foxes,	51
Order of exercise No 1	6
Order of exercise No 2	7
Praise the Lord,	72

Sending the light,	83
Stepping in the light,	79
Temperance,	111
The children who s..	72
The good Shepherd,	61
The Lord is good to a	18
The Sabbath day,	87
The use of the Bible.	108

Hood's Choir Journal
A Monthly Magazine

Containing anthems and selections for use in public worship. Enough material for all purposes will be found in the course of a year—Christmas, Easter, Thanksgiving, etc., are provided for. It is the aim of the editors to keep the grade of pieces within the compass of ordinary choirs, at same time keeping in mind that good melody and good harmony need not of necessity be technically difficult.

SUBSCRIBE NOW

One number, 75 cents per year
Five or more to one address, 50c. per year

Extra numbers, mailed, 10c. per copy

Any Chorister is entitled to one sample copy free

SWENEY'S Anthem Selections

196 pages, carefully selected gems by Palmer, Geibel, Entwisle, Sweney and many others. Condensed arrangements, so as to be easily performed; not too difficult for most volunteer choirs.

60 cents per copy, by mail ; $5.00 per dozen, by express.

The Organ Score
Anthem Book No. 2

By Jno. R. Sweney and W. J. Kirkpatrick
Same size and style as No. 1.

192 pages. Solid print, yet clear and easily read type. The anthems and other selections are of the best for church choirs.

60 cents, by mail ; $5.00 per dozen, by express

Heyser's Anthems

A collection of thirty melodious, practical anthems for chorus or quartet choirs. Moderate grade, effective and full of character.

30c. per copy ; $3.00 per dozen. postpaid.

Anthems and Voluntaries
FOR THE CHURCH CHOIR

By Jno. R. Sweney and Wm. J. Kirkpatrick

The standby of anthem books, too well and favorably known to require description. It is now issued in two sections, known as Section 1 and Section 2.

Price, 60c. each, by mail ; $5 per dozen, not mailed

The Gospel Chorus
FOR MALE VOICES

By Sweney, Kirkpatrick and O'Kane

Needs but to be known and your male quartet or chorus will not be without it. Nothing but vigorous gospel choruses, new or specially arranged, occupy its pages.

Price, by mail, 50c.; $5 per doz., not mailed

Gabriel's Anthems
By Chas. H. Gabriel

Contains 71 available pieces for church choirs. The work of this well-known author is always of high order; his anthem book is worthy of special commendation.

Price, 50c., by mail; $5 per doz., by express

Copies of above will be mailed to members of Music Committees on approval, or to any address on receipt of retail price

JOHN J. HOOD

PHILADELPHIA, 1024 Arch St.   CHICAGO, 38 Randolph St.

www.ingramcontent.com/pod-product-compliance
Lightning Source LLC
Chambersburg PA
CBHW030401170426
43202CB00010B/1450